Praise for **Don't Do Business with Dicks**

"In business, your biggest asset isn't just your product; it's the people you surround yourself with. David Meltzer gets it right: Success and decency aren't mutually exclusive. This book is a powerful reminder that who you do business with matters just as much as how you do it."

—Daymond John, CEO, FUBU and The Shark Group, and
TV Personality, ABC's *Shark Tank*

"This book is about more than business; it's about values. David's message hits home: You can win without cutting corners, and you can lead without losing who you are."

—Marshall Faulk, NFL Hall of Famer, Super Bowl Champion,
Entrepreneur, and Philanthropist

"Success in business starts with mindset and David reminds us that character is part of that equation. This book is a must-read for anyone who wants to lead with both intelligence and integrity."

—Jim Kwik, *New York Times* Bestselling Author, *Limitless*

"David Meltzer understands that emotional intelligence is a competitive advantage. *Don't Do Business with Dicks* is a powerful playbook for anyone who wants to build lasting relationships and lead with principle."

—Mike Tannenbaum, former NFL Executive;
Front Office Analyst, ESPN; and Founder, The 33rd Team

DON'T DO
BUSINESS
WITH DICKS

Also by David Meltzer

Connected to Goodness: Manifest Everything You Desire
in Business and Life
(with Harrison Lebowitz)

Compassionate Capitalism: Journey to the Soul of Business
(with Blaine Bartlett)

Be Unstoppable: How to Create the Life You Love
(with Jack Canfield and Cynthia Kersey)

Game-Time Decision Making: High-Scoring Business Strategies
from the Biggest Names in Sports

DON'T DO BUSINESS WITH DICKS

How to Ditch Toxicity and Align Yourself with Positive Influences

DAVID MELTZER

MATT
HOLT

Matt Holt Books
An Imprint of BenBella Books, Inc.
Dallas, TX

MATT HOLT BENBELLA

Matt Holt is an imprint of BenBella Books, Inc.
8080 N. Central Expressway
Suite 1700
Dallas, TX 75206
benbellabooks.com
Send feedback to feedback@benbellabooks.com

BenBella and *Matt Holt* are federally registered trademarks.

Printed in the United States of America
10 9 8 7 6 5 4 3 2 1

Library of Congress Control Number: 2025036185
ISBN 9781637748053 (hardcover)
ISBN 9781637748060 (electronic)

Editing by Greg Newton Brown
Copyediting by Michael Fedison
Proofreading by Martha Gallant and Sarah Vostok
Text design and composition by Jordan Koluch
Cover design by Brigid Pearson
Cover image © Adobe Stock / comicsans (AI generated)
Printed by Lake Book Manufacturing

Special discounts for bulk sales are available.
Please contact bulkorders@benbellabooks.com.

I dedicate this book and my journey to my beautiful wife
and lifesaver, Julie, and our four amazing children—
my M & Ms—Marissa, Mia, Marlena, and Miles.
I love you, I appreciate you, and I always have your back.

To my mother:

This book is a reflection of what you taught me.

To lead with kindness, to act with integrity,
and to always pursue a life of purpose over popularity.

I am healthy, I am happy, and I appreciate you.

Thank you for being my greatest teacher. I love you.

I miss you. I carry you with me, always.

Contents

Foreword

If you've ever spent any time around founders, you know one thing: founders love aphorisms. We love to take the entire universe of insight and wisdom and boil it down into a handful of pithy, one-sentence truths. Maybe it's out of efficiency, or maybe it's out of ego, but the best founders I've known in my life all communicate their worldview in "isms."

As a lifelong founder, I've got plenty of "isms" in my bag, but the one I always come back to is this:

A business is just people.

I say these five words at least once a week. In interviews. In board meetings. Onstage. It's the axiom I always come back to, because it's the one piece of truth that is always borne out, again and again.

Success has many fathers—anyone who's ever had any can tell you that. Timing matters. Strategy matters. Product-market fit . . . that matters too. But what matters more than anything is people.

When I look back and take stock of my entrepreneurial career, this is the throughline: People. I've had wins and losses, ups and downs. I cofounded two multibillion-dollar unicorns and several more outright failures. But when I find good people, I always find ways to work with them again—whatever the business outcome. "My entire career has been a search for cofounders" is one of my "isms" too. Because in the end, people are what matter.

That's why this book is so essential.

David Meltzer isn't just another business guy shouting about mindset. He's lived it. He's lost millions. He's rebuilt it all. And he's done it while consistently putting people and purpose first. David has sat at tables most people dream of: NFL front offices, Fortune 500 boardrooms, and media studios. And he'll tell you the same thing I will:

Being smart isn't enough. Being a good person matters more.

Whether it's a single startup or an entire society, prosperity is always downstream from culture. And I can tell you this from personal experience: it only takes one asshole to mess up a culture. One jerk can do far more damage than a hundred incompetents. A business is just people, and you have to choose your people carefully.

The title notwithstanding, this book isn't just a rant about jerks in business. If you want to read a rant about jerks in business, you can read my book (it's coming soon). But David isn't as petty as I am, so he's written something far more indispensable. It's a field guide for identifying the red flags early, protecting your energy, and building something meaningful with the right partners, investors, and collaborators. It's about setting a standard, not just for how others treat you, but for how you show up every day.

Whether you're a founder, an operator, an investor, or a dreamer, *Don't Do Business with Dicks* will give you the language, framework, and courage to build a career that's not only successful but sustainable and built on respect.

Read this book. Live by it. And remember, just because someone has money, influence, or experience doesn't mean they deserve your time or trust.

Let's build better.

—Josh Luber
Founder of ghostwrite, cofounder of Stock X & Fanatics Collectibles

Preface

In the world of business and competition, few stories are as riveting as my first day stepping into the chaotic whirlwind that was Leigh Steinberg's office. Imagine it: Leigh Steinberg, the legendary sports agent who inspired Tom Cruise's iconic character in *Jerry Maguire* and helped popularize the unforgettable catchphrase, "Show me the money!" I arrived as the new chief operations officer, ready to take on any challenge thrown my way. But what I found was a company teetering on the brink of disaster.

The moment I walked through those doors, I could sense the tension hanging heavily in the air. The agency was embroiled in a significant deal—negotiating to bring the NFL's St. Louis Rams back to Los Angeles with a staggering $900 million price tag. Yet, there was something else beneath the surface, an unease that no one dared name. I felt like I'd walked onto the stage of a play where every actor knew their lines except me. It didn't take long before I discovered the lead actor, Leigh himself, would not be appearing anytime soon.

A secretary, with hesitation lacing her voice, finally spilled the truth. Leigh, an icon in his field, was not absent due to some minor illness or personal matter as I might have wished in those first panicked moments. No, he'd been arrested for public drunkenness just the day prior and was now in a court-ordered detox program. His absence wasn't a temporary hiccup; it was a chasm that threatened to swallow the entire agency if quick action wasn't taken.

There I was, thrust unexpectedly into the spotlight, expected to finalize negotiations that could make or break not only the company but also the professional careers of everyone within it. And let's not sugarcoat this: Buying an NFL team is not your everyday business deal. This required playing in a league I had never so much as watched from the stands. I wasn't the guy who finalized massive deals yet. My mind was racing. Leigh needed solutions and fast. I was able to get Leigh on the phone for a moment. There was no time for an in-depth plan, and Leigh wasn't exactly in a place to deliver one anyway. His instructions were simple yet profound, articulated with the clarity of someone who had sobered up enough to get straight to the point.

He said, "David, always be fair. Don't negotiate to the last penny, and don't do business with dicks."

We were dealing with a company called Franklin Financial. The bid was for $900 million. Bringing professional football back to Los Angeles, a huge market with a long history of high-caliber professional sports, was at stake. Talk about being out over your skis. Talk about being thrown into the fire. In my very first week running the most notable sports agency in the world, I was searching for what to do.

Leigh's words settled over me like a mantra I have carried to this day.

What initially seemed like a simplistic directive soon became a guiding philosophy, not just for negotiating high-stakes deals, but for navigating life itself. This distilled wisdom became my compass as I embarked on what would become one of the most challenging chapters of my career.

Over the years, these principles have proven invaluable. I've since negotiated more than $2 billion in contracts and agreements—not by being ruthless or cunning, but by being principled and kind. They say that life in competitive fields such as sales, marketing, management, entertainment, and media is a relentless battlefield, rife with treachery and conflict. But what if that didn't need to be true? What if the key to success and fulfillment lay not in outsmarting opponents but in choosing kindness, gratitude, and accountability?

The Rams did indeed end up back in Los Angeles, in large part due to Leigh's advice and my action.

And now here I am with you, sharing and expanding on the advice that changed my life.

This book seeks to turn that "what if" into "what is." Together, we will explore why surrounding yourself with the right people matters more than having all the answers. We'll delve into how living with forgiveness and gratitude can transform not only your career but your entire outlook on life. You'll come to understand the importance of staying "above the line"—a mindset that breeds responsibility and banishes victimhood, paving the way for meaningful connections and flourishing careers.

This book unfolds in three parts, each building on the last. Part 1, "The Power of Right," explores the foundational idea that success starts with making the right choices—surrounding yourself with the right people, being the right kind of person, seeking out the right environments, and operating from a place of moral clarity and intention in embodying right business practices. Drawing inspiration from both hard-earned experience and timeless wisdom, this section unpacks what it means to act with integrity in every corner of your life and work. Part 2, "Own Your Time, Own Your Life," shifts focus to your relationship with time—arguably your most precious resource. We'll look at how to stop feeling owned by the clock and start using time to live and lead more meaningfully. Finally, part 3, "Living the Four Great Truths," brings it all together, guiding you in how to embody the deeper values of empathy and forgiveness, gratitude, accountability, and effective communication. These four truths aren't just traits—they're practices that, when lived, can transform your business, your relationships, and your sense of self.

The chapters ahead are filled with actionable insights and anecdotes drawn from both my personal experiences and those of others who have excelled at balancing life and business and doing good work the right way. Here, you'll find real-world lessons to help you cultivate your own "gold standard" in personal and professional dealings.

So, whether you're at the dawn of your professional journey or standing at its twilight—whether you've crossed paths with difficult personalities or been the difficult one yourself (I know I've lived both roles through the years)—know that change is possible. You can build a career rooted in happiness and kindness, one where you work with integrity and alongside others who share your vision. Let's embark on this journey together and discover how to fill your life with the right people, ideas, places, and opportunities, leaving behind the negativity and pettiness that stunt growth.

By the end of this book, armed with these new perspectives and tools, you'll be empowered to rid your life of toxic influences, welcoming in the right people, ideas, places, and opportunities, and learning to start leaving behind the negativity and pettiness that stunt growth. You'll no longer find yourself entangled with those who seek only to stall your progress. Instead, you'll stand strong and focused, poised to achieve success in a manner that honors both your ambitions and your values.

Welcome to a new way of doing business, where success and decency aren't mutually exclusive, but rather, go hand in hand. It's time to show the world—and maybe even yourself—that being good isn't just possible; it's profitable.

PART 1

THE POWER OF RIGHT

PART 1

THE POWER OF RIGHT

Chapter 1

DICKS, DICKS EVERYWHERE

Surround Yourself with the Right People

Before I could understand the importance of surrounding myself with the right people, I had to face a brutal truth: I was becoming someone I didn't like. That truth came from my wife—who had every reason to walk away but chose not to. Instead, she gave me a single ultimatum: If we were going to build something better together, I had to cut ties with my three closest friends. These were guys I'd known for years. They weren't bad people—but when I was with them, I became someone I didn't want to be. The drinking, the decisions, the direction of my life—it was all off course, and it wasn't who I wanted to be in this life. Saying goodbye to them wasn't easy. I told each one, "This isn't about you. It's about me. I don't like who I am when I'm with you." That moment changed everything. It was the first time I truly understood how deeply we are shaped—fed and bled—by the people we keep closest.

Navigating the complex world of professional relationships is much like journeying through a crowded cityscape, where encounters with challenging personalities are inevitable. It's not just about avoiding these figures but learning how to skillfully maneuver them to cultivate a network that uplifts and inspires. In today's fast-paced environments, especially in competitive fields such as sales, marketing, and media, professionals often find themselves surrounded by a mix of personalities. Each interaction can either be a stepping stone toward personal growth or an obstacle to progress. The key lies in distinguishing which connections to foster and which to approach with caution. Developing this discerning eye isn't automatic; it requires an understanding of oneself and a commitment to surrounding oneself with those who reflect your values and ambitions.

This chapter delves into practical strategies for building meaningful professional and personal relationships that align with your core values. It addresses the significance of self-awareness as the foundation for all other interactions. By embracing concepts like gratitude, empathy, accountability, and effective communication, individuals can craft a space that naturally attracts supportive, like-minded allies. These qualities act as a filter, helping to identify those whose contributions enhance rather than detract from their lives. Readers will learn how personal integrity plays a critical role in setting the tone for these relationships and why happiness derived from alignment with your values creates a welcoming aura for positive influences.

Beyond interpersonal dynamics, this chapter also provides insight into maintaining balance amid competing workplace pressures, reinforcing the importance of integrity and resilience in nurturing professional respect and admiration. As you read on, you'll uncover tools and techniques to help navigate the often tricky terrain of personal and professional networks, ensuring your circle consists of individuals who not only resonate with your mission but also propel you toward greater achievements.

Meeting the Four Great Truths

Building a strong relationship with oneself is pivotal in establishing meaningful connections with others. It's not just about liking who you are; it's cultivating a deep, unwavering respect for yourself that forms the cornerstone of all other relationships. Think about it this way: When you treat yourself with kindness and honesty, you set the standard for how others should treat you too.

Before we go further, I want to acknowledge the four core values (the Four Great Truths) that shape every relationship I build—empathy and forgiveness, gratitude, accountability, and effective communication. These traits act like a magnet, pulling the right people into your orbit. We'll explore them in depth later in the book, especially in part 3, but keep them in mind as we begin laying the foundation for attracting people who align with your purpose.

Imagine these qualities as traits that pull people toward you, much like a magnet. Gratitude, for instance, isn't just about saying thank you; it's a mindset that recognizes and appreciates the contributions of others, creating an environment where people feel valued. Empathy goes beyond understanding someone's words; it's about truly comprehending their feelings and perspectives, leading to deeper, more authentic connections.

Accountability is another pillar, often underappreciated yet profoundly impactful. When you hold yourself accountable for your actions and decisions, it demonstrates integrity and reliability. People are drawn to those who take responsibility, as it fosters trust and mutual respect. Lastly, effective communication ties these elements together. It's not just about speaking clearly—it involves listening actively and engaging thoughtfully, ensuring that each interaction brings clarity and connection rather than confusion and conflict.

Bringing these truths into our daily interactions isn't a checkbox exercise. It's a commitment to live authentically and engage with others from a place of sincerity. As one embodies gratitude, empathy, accountability, and effective communication, there's a noticeable shift in the quality of people they attract. These qualities act as a filtering mechanism, drawing individuals who share similar values and aspirations into your life.

Here's a key guideline: Attract the right people by being accountable and honest. Embracing accountability means acknowledging mistakes without deflection and being dependable in fulfilling promises. Honesty, on the other hand, speaks to transparency in motives and actions, fostering environments where trust can flourish. When you're committed to these values, you'll find that you attract individuals who mirror them, creating a network of supportive, like-minded allies.

Personal integrity and happiness are fundamental in influencing the quality of connections we make throughout our lives. Integrity isn't just about having moral principles; it's about ensuring your actions align with your stated beliefs. When these are congruent, it becomes easier to develop trustful and enduring relationships because others view you as consistent and trustworthy.

Happiness plays an equally vital role here. Happiness is not simply about constant euphoria or pleasure; it's a state of contentment and satisfaction with life. When you're genuinely happy, it becomes a contagious energy that affects how other people perceive and interact with you. Your joy can inspire those around you, creating a positive cycle of uplifting exchanges and experiences.

When one lives in alignment with their core values and pursues genuine happiness, it sends a powerful message about what they will accept in their life. By setting boundaries aligned with personal integrity, it effectively sifts out negative energies or personalities that don't resonate with your vision. Personal integrity isn't just about ethics; it's an essential tool in curating a fulfilling social environment.

In professional settings, especially in competitive fields like sales, marketing, and sports, maintaining such values can be both challenging and rewarding. The pressure to conform or compromise might arise; however, staying true to your principles often garners respect and admiration from peers and colleagues—even adversaries.

It's crucial to remember that these aren't finite goals but ongoing practices. Every day presents new opportunities to practice gratitude, refine empathetic interaction, uphold accountability, and communicate effectively. Through continuous dedication to these ideals, individuals gradually construct a robust foundation for all present and future relationships, ensuring they are both meaningful and resilient.

Relativity and Managing Difficult Family Dynamics

Choosing the right people is hard enough in business. In families, where you don't always have a choice, it can feel nearly impossible. I learned this firsthand early in my career—when my desire to do right by my family collided with the reality that love doesn't always equal good advice.

When I graduated from law school during a recession, I was lucky to have two job offers. One was what my mother called a "real lawyer" job—an oil and gas litigator position with a generous $150,000 salary. The other was a sales role with West Publishing, the company that had just launched Westlaw. It came with a $250,000 comp plan and a chance to ride the wave of something brand new: the internet. My heart was with the sales role. I wanted to take care of my mom, buy her a house and a car—ease the burden I'd watched her carry for years. So I asked her what she thought.

She didn't hesitate: "You need to be a real lawyer. That internet thing? It's a fad. Nobody will ever use it."

She said it out of love. But it was love tangled with fear—fear for my security, fear of the unknown, fear of losing me to a world she didn't understand. I've never forgotten that moment. It taught me a lesson I carry with me to this day: Just because someone loves you doesn't mean their advice is rooted in what's right for you. Especially in family, people may care deeply and still steer you wrong—because they're projecting their fears, not your future.

Whether you're navigating the competitive worlds of sales, media, entrepreneurship, or another field entirely, personal relationships can often become collateral damage. And among those, family dynamics may present the most enduring and complex challenges. Understanding how to maneuver these relationships through the lens of relativity can offer perspective, preserve empathy, and protect your emotional well-being.

Adopting Einstein's theory of relativity in this context doesn't mean applying physics directly but rather recognizing that everything is shaped by point of view. Our perceptions and reactions are filtered through personal experience. Realizing this can help explain why family members may act in ways that seem controlling, dismissive, or even hurtful. Their behavior is often not about you—it's about what they've lived through. That awareness can create emotional distance without severing ties.

Managing family dynamics consciously means being deliberate about how we engage. Just as a seasoned marketer would strategically plan a campaign, you can thoughtfully shape your responses. Conscious interaction involves setting boundaries while remaining open to others' perspectives. If a sibling always brings up conflict at family dinners, for example, it may help to pull them aside and express a desire to focus on what connects you, not what divides you. In challenging family relationships, empathy and graciousness are key. Being gracious doesn't mean accepting mistreatment. It means choosing to highlight what's working, however small. If a family member frequently focuses on the negative, notice the moments they offer support or express care. Those glimpses of kindness can be anchors.

This practice doesn't happen overnight. But consistently applying perspective, empathy, and conscious boundaries can build emotional resilience. Consider journaling your reactions to family interactions. Over time, patterns will emerge—revealing growth, and helping you recalibrate when old wounds get triggered.

Relativity reminds us that every person's reality is shaped by their history. When we approach family through this lens, it opens space for patience and compassion—even when advice is misguided or actions feel unfair. In cases where abuse or emotional harm is present, this understanding doesn't mean staying in harm's way. It means giving yourself permission to seek help, create space, and build safety elsewhere.

Responding to criticism with calm, even kindness, can disarm conflict and preserve dignity. Gratitude, even in the hardest relationships, can help you move forward—not by excusing pain, but by valuing what you've learned from it.

Family isn't always where you find the "right people." But even in those relationships, you can practice the same discernment and integrity that guides you elsewhere in life. And when you do, you'll be better prepared to find, and choose, the people who truly belong in your circle.

Critical Life Relationships and Balance

In the labyrinth of professional life, identifying and nurturing relationships that contribute to our personal and career balance can be just as essential as mastering our trades. A pivotal relationship check starts at the core of what fulfills us—our jobs, homes, and personal connections. Imagine your work environment. Ideally, it should be a place where you feel productive and appreciated for your skills—a fulfilling job is more than a paycheck; it's a source of satisfaction and self-worth. It's crucial to seek roles or projects that align with your values and aspirations, providing not only financial stability but emotional fulfillment. Picture a marketer passionately crafting campaigns that resonate with their ethos or an entrepreneur leading ventures that mirror their dreams. A job that nurtures your drive can significantly boost your life's balance.

Just as essential—but often even more complex—is choosing a supportive spouse or partner whose presence becomes a pillar in your pursuit of happiness. Healthy relationships don't just happen. They require shared values, honest communication, and a willingness to grow together. I've learned that partnership isn't about perfection—it's about alignment. It's about choosing someone who challenges you to be better without making you feel like you're not enough. Sometimes the hardest part is recognizing when a relationship isn't supportive—when you're constantly sacrificing your own peace just to keep things calm. Defining your own boundaries, expectations, and nonnegotiables becomes critical. The right partner doesn't just cheer for your success—they help build the foundation that allows it.

Some of the best life advice I've ever received came from my grandfather. He told me there are three things you need to be happy. First, you need one intimate partner that you love and who loves you. That partner becomes the liaison to all your other relationships—friends, family, work. You'll spend a third of your life with those people, and if you're not grounded in a loving partnership, that third suffers. Second, you need to love what you do—the activity you get paid for. If you're working for a third of your life and you hate your work, that's another third gone. And finally, a third of your life is spent sleeping and schlepping—so buy the best bed you can find. That's it. Love who you're with. Love what you do. And sleep well.

Whether sharing everyday moments or weathering storms together, having someone who genuinely supports your ambitions can create a harmonious home environment. This doesn't mean perfection is expected, but rather, finding someone whose imperfections you are willing to embrace and vice versa. Consider renowned actors or athletes whose successes often mirror the support they receive from their partners. Remember, maintaining a solid relationship requires continuous effort, open communication, and compromise, contributing to both personal contentment and professional resilience.

We often talk about surrounding ourselves with the right people—those who uplift us, challenge us, and align with our values. But there's another, often-overlooked relationship that shapes every part of your life: your relationship with rest. In my experience, the most grounded and effective people I know don't just work hard—they protect their energy. And they respect when others do the same.

I've learned that when you're building a life filled with good people, rest is what allows you to keep showing up as your best self. A good bed, a peaceful environment, and quality sleep aren't luxuries—they're your foundation. When you're constantly drained, even the best relationships start to fray. But when you prioritize rest, you think more clearly, connect more deeply, and show up more intentionally for the people who matter most.

Beyond these foundational elements, the circle of friends we choose reflects our values and influences our journey. Friendships, unlike familial bonds, are chosen—they're deliberate connections based on shared interests, perspectives, and experiences. When selecting friends, it's essential to assess the mutual benefits and understand the capacity for growth within these relationships. Finding friends who encourage professional development while offering emotional support can make a significant difference. Consider the friendships formed through networks like alumni associations or professional groups where shared goals foster dynamic interactions that enhance both personal and professional lives.

In business, distinguishing between associates becomes particularly important. Not all colleagues will share your passion or dedication, so aligning yourself with those driven by similar enthusiasms can lead to greater professional growth.

Collaborating with like-minded individuals often results in synergies where creativity and productivity flourish. A manager might find mentorship in a passionate director, learning valuable insights that propel career advancement. Conversely, surrounding oneself with unmotivated or negative influences can hinder progress and dampen spirits. Take inspiration from partnerships seen in successful enterprises where synergy among team members drives innovation and success, proving that teamwork truly makes the dream work.

Ultimately, building and maintaining these pivotal relationships requires intentionality and discernment. Reflect on what matters most to you and assess whether your current relationships align with those priorities. Are you surrounded by people who elevate you or pull you down? Like any worthwhile endeavor, fostering meaningful connections demands time, patience, and commitment. Regularly evaluate your interactions, considering whether they contribute to or detract from your life balance. Don't be afraid to let go of toxic relationships or distance yourself from those who don't align with your vision.

Moreover, embracing diversity—be it in thoughts, backgrounds, or experiences—within your circles can offer fresh perspectives and broaden your horizons. Diverse teams often outperform homogeneous ones due to varied viewpoints and approaches, leading to innovative solutions.

Whether in friendships or work partnerships, valuing different perspectives enriches your own understanding and enhances problem-solving abilities.

As you navigate this journey, remain open to adjustments. Life's ebb and flow may shift your needs and wants over time, requiring reevaluation of what constitutes an ideal relationship. Being flexible and adaptive ensures that you can effectively manage change and continue growing personally and professionally. Trust your instincts when it comes to relationships, relying on intuition to guide you toward those who bring out the best in you.

The Role of Mentors in Personal Development

Mentorship has shaped some of the most meaningful and unexpected moments of my life. One of my earliest experiences with this came long before I understood what mentorship even was.

When I was 10 years old, growing up in Akron, Ohio, I dreamed of going to the Rose Bowl. My two favorite teams were Ohio State—and whoever was playing Michigan. In 1978, Michigan was playing Washington, and Washington's quarterback was a young man named Warren Moon. I begged my mom to go. As a single mother of six kids, it wasn't easy. But to my surprise, she said yes. What I didn't realize was that my mom, not being a football fan, thought I meant the *Rose Bowl Parade*—not the game.

So there I was, watching floats roll down the street, counting the minutes until kickoff, when I said, "I can't wait for the game." She turned to me and said, "We're not going to the game—we can't afford it."

Instead, I listened to the game on my AM radio during the drive home, hanging on every play. Against all odds as a 16½-point underdog, Washington, led by Warren Moon, took a stunning victory over powerhouse Michigan. Moon was named MVP of the Rose Bowl in his hometown of Los Angeles. I never forgot that. I admired him long before I ever met him.

Years later, Warren Moon became not only my business partner but one of my closest friends—and a true mentor. I've shared life and business with him in ways I never could have imagined as a kid. One night, I was honored at an Angels game where I'd been invited to throw the first pitch in front of a sold-out crowd of 62,000 on Sombrero Night. I was nervous—maybe more nervous than I've ever been. Warren put his arm around me and taught me about the majesty of calmness. He told me to breathe in through my nose and out through my mouth, and to aim high. I told him I planned to throw a knuckleball so I'd have an excuse if it went wild. He laughed and said, "Do your best. Go have fun."

I threw a strike, knuckleball and all—with Warren cheering from the sidelines. It was a dream come true.

Mentorship is more than just guidance; it's a pathway to unlocking our true potential in both personal and professional realms. The significance of having mentors cannot be overstated. Surrounding oneself with knowledgeable and experienced individuals fosters an atmosphere of learning and growth, which is crucial for anyone seeking to excel in their field.

Having a diverse set of mentors provides a broader perspective on various challenges and opportunities. Each mentor brings unique insights that can help tailor guidance to fit specific aspirations. When you engage with multiple mentors, you're exposed to a wealth of knowledge across different industries and experiences. This diversity enriches your understanding and equips you with a tool kit of strategies applicable to different scenarios. For instance, a mentor specializing in marketing may offer innovative tactics to boost brand visibility, while another from the financial sector can provide strategies for efficient budgeting and investment.

It's essential, however, to approach mentorship with clarity and purpose. Successful mentoring goes beyond just seeking advice—it's about clearly defining why you're pursuing mentorship and what you hope to achieve. Before approaching potential mentors, take the time to assess your goals. Are you looking to improve leadership skills? Perhaps you're interested in transitioning to a new industry or need support in navigating a complex work environment. By pinpointing these objectives beforehand, you can identify mentors whose expertise aligns with your aspirations, ensuring a mutually beneficial relationship.

Recognition of a mentor's potential impact is also vital. Consider the qualities and experiences of potential mentors that resonate most with your personal and professional journey. Steve Wynn, renowned for his contributions to the casino and hospitality industries, exemplifies how targeted mentorship can lead to monumental achievements. His ability to envision luxury resorts that transformed Las Vegas is partly credited to mentors who nurtured his creativity and strategic thinking. By aligning with mentors who understood his vision and business model, Wynn was able to push boundaries and set new standards within his industry.

Similarly, Greg S. Reid, a successful author and entrepreneur, highlights the transformative power of mentorship in achieving our dreams. Reid leverages relationships with mentors who are experts in fields he aspires to excel in. This strategic alignment has enabled him to maximize opportunities for personal growth and professional success. His journey underscores the importance of choosing mentors whose experiences and values complement your own, creating a synergy that fosters empowerment and progression.

For those looking to embark on this path, valuing mentors involves active engagement and open communication. Show genuine interest in their stories and learnings, and don't hesitate to share your progress, challenges, and reflections. The dynamic exchange not only strengthens the mentor–mentee bond but also creates an enriching collaborative process that benefits both parties.

Choosing the right mentors often entails considering their availability and willingness to engage meaningfully. Quality over quantity matters here—select mentors who have the capacity and desire to invest time and resources into your development. Effective mentors are also those who challenge you to think critically, encourage you to step outside your comfort zone, and offer constructive feedback to guide your continued improvement.

When tapping into a network of mentors, it's valuable to appreciate the distinctive roles each plays. Some may serve as industry experts, offering technical advice and insider knowledge. Others might act as strategic thinkers, assisting you in crafting long-term career plans and identifying growth opportunities. Emotional supporters can be just as crucial, providing encouragement and motivation during challenging times. Understanding and leveraging these varied roles ensures you gain comprehensive support in all facets of your personal and professional life.

Looking back, I often think about that moment on the sidelines with Warren. What made it so powerful wasn't just his football legacy or business acumen—it was his calm presence, his belief in me, and his willingness to share something simple but profound: breathe, aim high, and enjoy it. That's mentorship at its best. It's not about giving someone all the answers. It's about helping them trust themselves enough to take the shot.

Additionally, one should not underestimate the importance of giving back to the mentorship relationship. While mentors share their wisdom and experience, mentees can contribute by offering fresh perspectives, acknowledging their mentors' contributions, and extending support where possible. This reciprocal relationship enhances mutual respect and lays the groundwork for sustained engagement.

In today's interconnected world, finding mentors has become more accessible than ever. Social media, professional networks, and industry conferences provide platforms to connect with potential mentors. However, remember that genuine relationships stem from authentic interactions. Focus on building connections based on shared interests and values rather than merely ticking off names on a list.

To truly harness the power of mentorship, continuous learning is key. Approach each interaction with curiosity and openness to new ideas. Be willing to adapt and evolve as you incorporate lessons learned into your personal and professional practices. Over time, these cumulative insights will shape you into a more effective leader and collaborator, capable of making informed decisions and driving positive change within your sphere of influence.

Self-Love and Attracting Positive Influences

In the hustle and bustle of our professional lives, there's a profound truth that often gets sidelined: the power of self-love. This isn't just about pampering oneself or indulging in temporary pleasures; it's about a deep-seated belief in your own worth. Believing in yourself doesn't just change how you feel—it acts like a magnet, drawing supportive and genuine individuals into your life across family, friendships, and professional circles.

Years ago, I mentored a young entrepreneur who had all the pieces in place—talent, drive, funding—but couldn't stop second-guessing his worth. We built in simple practices: daily gratitude, intentional self-talk, and asking, "What makes me feel aligned today?" Six months later, his business was thriving—but more importantly, his energy had shifted. He was surrounded by better people. Better clients. He even reconnected with his father, who said, "You feel different now." That's the compounding power of self-love: One positive influence draws in another, and then another.

Consider the moments when you've encountered someone who exudes confidence and self-assurance. Their presence is captivating, not because they shout about their achievements, but because they carry themselves with a quiet dignity. That kind of self-belief tends to attract similar energy. In the workplace, such individuals find themselves surrounded by colleagues who support rather than compete destructively. Within families, they become pillars of strength. In friendships, they become the anchor during turbulent times.

To consistently draw positive people into our lives, gratitude and empathy must be practiced diligently. These aren't just buzzwords but tools capable of transforming environments. Imagine walking into an office where appreciation is part of the culture. When gratitude is expressed regularly, relationships flourish. Empathy bridges differences, allowing us to see through another's lens and respond with compassion and understanding.

Reflection Prompt

- Who are the five people you spend the most time with?
- Which of those relationships energize you—and which ones drain you?
- What are three small ways you can better protect your energy this week?

Self-love doesn't just change how you feel. It shapes who shows up in your life—and who no longer fits. The modern world bombards us with messages equating success with material wealth and status. However, when we align ourselves with these superficial preoccupations, we risk forming connections based on external attributes rather than genuine compatibility. True relationships thrive not on what people possess but on who people are.

When we endeavor to cultivate self-love without being tethered to materialistic measures, we create space for authentic connections. Have you ever noticed how conversations at social gatherings often revolve around accomplishments or acquisitions? Steering clear of such narratives and focusing instead on personal values invites deeper, more meaningful exchanges. This redirection allows you to connect with others on shared beliefs and passions rather than superficial markers of success.

Consider the stories of those who shifted focus away from the allure of prestige toward self-awareness and authenticity. These individuals often find their personal and professional networks enriched with people who resonate with their core values. By choosing companions based on honesty and mutual respect instead of societal accolades, the relationships that form are naturally supportive and enduring.

As a professional navigating complex industries and workplaces, it's essential to remember that the company you keep significantly influences your growth. Surrounding yourself with people who reflect your values and encourage your self-worth enhances both personal satisfaction and career progression. Finding mentors, peers, and friends who appreciate your authentic self rather than your title or income cultivates a nurturing ground for personal and professional fulfillment.

Embracing self-love through actions like cultivating the right people and filtering the dicks out of your life is an ongoing journey about valuing personal achievements and learning to face setbacks with resilience. Each step builds the inner confidence that draws more of what you want into your life. By embracing gratitude and empathy, you actively transform your internal and external worlds, inviting those who will genuinely celebrate your successes and stand by you during challenges.

Final Insights

In this chapter, we explored the powerful idea that surrounding yourself with the right people—and filtering out the wrong ones—starts from within. By fostering qualities like gratitude, empathy, accountability, and effective communication, you naturally begin to attract individuals who align with your values. When you're confident in your identity and purpose, it's easier to create transparent, genuine connections. And when your actions align with your beliefs, that's integrity—and others can feel it.

Self-love and happiness also matter more than we sometimes admit. They act as magnets, drawing in the kind of energy that sustains—not drains—you. The journey of building and maintaining meaningful relationships isn't a onetime fix. It's a daily commitment to showing up as your best self and surrounding yourself with those who help you stay that way.

Guidelines

- Embrace gratitude and empathy as everyday practices.
- Acknowledge small victories and express appreciation to those around you.
- When disagreements arise, take a step back to understand differing perspectives.

Developing these habits enriches your interactions and shapes a more cohesive environment.

Takeaways

- Right people reflect right values—your values.
- Personal integrity is your strongest filter.
- Self-love isn't selfish—it's strategic.
- Gratitude and empathy are relationship accelerators.
- You don't rise alone—your circle helps lift you.

Ask Yourself

- Who in my life makes me feel more like myself when I'm around them?
- When was the last time I showed genuine appreciation for someone in my circle?
- What kind of energy am I giving off? Do I feel like someone others would want to be around?

All of what we've learned only works if you can learn to filter out negative influences. I was blessed to have my wife help show me that lesson. Here's a simple framework to help you assess who belongs in your life:

- **Check the Energy Exchange:** Do you feel drained or energized after being with them?
- **Watch for Blame and Gossip:** People who never take responsibility or constantly criticize others aren't safe collaborators.
- **Set Boundaries Early:** Say no with kindness, but with

clarity. Those who respect your boundaries are the ones worth keeping.

As we close this chapter, I can't help but think back to where it all started—with my wife's ultimatum. It was a brutal truth wrapped in love: If I wanted to grow, I had to let go. Setting a boundary with my three closest friends wasn't about them—it was about me choosing who I wanted to become. That decision set everything else in motion. Because when you clear out what no longer serves you, you make room for the people—and possibilities—that do.

In the next chapter, we'll explore the environments that shape us. Because it's not just who you surround yourself with—it's where you choose to stand.

Chapter 2

DON'T HANG LIKE A DICK

Surround Yourself with the Right Environments

Throughout my life, I've continually found that environments either elevate or erode you.

Where you spend most of your day plays a crucial role in shaping who you are and how you evolve. Whether it's your office, your team, or your social circle, the spaces (and the relationships that happen within those spaces) that we choose to immerse ourselves in can either propel us toward success or hold us back from reaching our full potential. Each decision about where you invest your time and energy creates a ripple effect on your career trajectory and personal development.

I used to think success came down to symbols. For me, that symbol was a Ferrari. I dreamed of owning one for years, and when I finally bought it, I thought I'd arrived. People would know I was successful. Women would notice. I was so lost back then I carried a picture of the car in my wallet—this was before phones—just so I could show it off.

When I started dating my wife, she nearly broke up with me over that picture. And looking back, I don't blame her. I didn't buy the Ferrari because I loved cars. I bought it because I wanted to be respected. I wanted people to think I was rich.

But the car turned out to be a pain. If I drove it too little, it broke down. If I drove it too much, it broke down. I couldn't park it near other cars for fear of scratches. And worst of all, it didn't make people admire me—it made them assume I was a jerk.

That car wasn't just a purchase. It was part of an environment I was building—one based on perception, not purpose. The car, the image, the people I was trying to impress—they were all part of a version of success that didn't align with who I really wanted to be. I'd surrounded myself with the wrong signals, and they were shaping my reputation, my energy, and even how I saw myself.

Years later, I was asked to keynote Career Day at a school in Beverly Hills. I pulled up in the Ferrari, parked illegally, gave my speech, and as I left, I overheard a kid say, "There goes that asshole with the Ferrari." That was me. Years after that, I was invited back again—but this time, things had changed. I drove a Chevy Volt, parked legally, walked to the school, and gave a speech about gratitude and purpose. On my way back, a student pointed and said, "Hey, there goes the gratitude guy."

That moment meant more to me than any car ever could. Because what you drive, wear, or flaunt won't define your worth—how you show up does. And more often than not, your environment reflects your values, whether you're aware of it or not.

Throughout this chapter, we'll dive into the profound impact that purposeful environments have on both personal satisfaction and professional achievement. We'll explore how aligning your surroundings with your values fosters clarity, confidence, and the kind of energy that sustains you—while filtering out what doesn't. From curating the spaces you work in to rethinking what you keep around you and why, this chapter will explore how to create environments that support who you are—and who you're becoming. The goal isn't just to find places that feel good, but to build surroundings that bring out your best and help you do the same for others.

Purposeful Work Environment

Consider the impact of spending 40-plus hours each week in an environment that doesn't resonate with your core values. The disconnect could lead to feelings of frustration and stagnation. On the other hand, when your work reflects what you genuinely care about, it provides a sense of fulfillment that transcends mere financial gain. This alignment not only boosts morale but also enhances productivity, fostering an atmosphere where progress becomes more attainable than perfection.

For instance, think about those who have discovered their careers in the realms of sports and entertainment. Whether they're athletes, actors, or agents, their professions often align closely with their passions and talents. This alignment serves as a powerful driver, enabling them to face challenges with resilience and creativity. Similarly, professionals in management and media find motivation in the sense of purpose derived from their roles, which directly connect to their larger career goals.

The concept of "persistence of perspective" emerges as a vital guideline in maintaining focus on long-term objectives. Persistence of perspective is the ability to keep your larger vision in mind even when the day-to-day feels discouraging or unclear. In fast-moving industries, setbacks are inevitable. But the key to overcoming them lies in your ability to zoom out—refocusing on where you're going rather than getting stuck in where you are. By developing the habit of shifting your perspective toward future goals, you build resilience against the noise and frustration of daily disappointments.

I know persistence of perspective because I lived without it for years. Early in my career, I tied success to status. I thought if I drove the right car, closed the right deal, or impressed the right people, I'd feel whole. But when the sales didn't come—or when the admiration I craved turned into judgment—I felt like a failure. What shifted everything was learning to zoom out. I stopped chasing the illusion of "arrived" and started focusing on who I wanted to become. Each deal I lost wasn't a verdict—it was a rep. A chance to get better, to realign, to move closer to something sustainable. That's persistence of perspective: the discipline to keep your long-term vision in focus, even when today punches you in the gut.

And here's where environment matters: The spaces and people around you either reinforce that bigger picture—or pull you back into the noise of ego, pressure, and distraction. The right environment doesn't just support your goals. It protects your perspective.

Equally important is recognizing that engaging in work you love encourages innovation. When passion fuels your endeavors, you find yourself willingly going the extra mile, exploring creative solutions to problems, and achieving results beyond expectations. This intrinsic motivation is a cornerstone of success across all professional domains.

A practical example is seen in entrepreneurs who launch startups based on ideas they are deeply passionate about. Their commitment to their vision propels them forward, even when faced with harsh market realities or financial constraints. This inner drive, born out of a strong connection to their work, often becomes a critical factor in the survival and eventual success of their ventures.

However, choosing work aligned with personal values is not without its challenges. It requires introspection and self-awareness to truly understand what drives you. Asking questions like "What do I value most?" and "What kind of impact do I want to make through my work?" can provide clarity. Additionally, surrounding yourself with environments and people that support your ambitions is crucial. This not only reinforces your dedication but also creates a network of support that nurtures personal and professional growth.

Given the importance of this alignment, it's beneficial to seek opportunities that allow for ongoing learning and development. Industries are constantly evolving, and staying engaged in your field means adapting to new trends and technologies. This adaptability is easier when you are sincerely interested in your work, making personal development feel less like an obligation and more like an exciting journey.

Professionals in media and journalism, for example, thrive on their curiosity and commitment to truth-telling. Their enthusiasm for uncovering stories and sharing knowledge keeps them continuously motivated, driving them to adapt and grow alongside the ever-changing landscape of the industry.

Ultimately, choosing work that aligns with your personal values and aspirations does more than support your career—it shapes the environment you live and grow in every day. When your surroundings reflect who you are and what you believe in, they reinforce the mindset you need to stay focused, adaptable, and fulfilled. That's the real power of persistence of perspective: creating conditions—both internal and external—that help you keep showing up for your purpose, even when the path gets messy. When your values shape your environment, your environment starts to protect your vision.

Persistence Beyond Challenges: Know Your Delta

Persistence plays a pivotal role in turning challenges into opportunities, especially within the high-pressure environments of sales, marketing, advertising, and entrepreneurship. But persistence is about more than just pushing through. It's about how you show up—consistently, imperfectly, and with intention—even when the outcome isn't guaranteed.

One of the greatest experiences of my life was playing college football. I use the word "play" loosely. I was an average Division III football player—actually, I later learned I was below average. But I loved it. And people often ask me, "What's the closest you've come to reaching your potential?" My honest answer? Playing below-average college football. Because my basement—my starting point in terms of skill—was so low that the distance I traveled just to compete was the greatest delta of my life.

I knew I wasn't going to start. I knew I was risking injury. But I went every day. I learned to love the reps. I learned to love what I didn't love. I learned to do the things other people wouldn't. And I kept showing up. That mindset—what I now call being "consistently persistent without quit"—became my foundation when I started selling legal research out of law school. Except this time, my basement was higher. I had skills. I had confidence. And when I applied that same persistent mindset, I outperformed everyone around me—three times over—and became a millionaire within nine months of graduating. The formula hadn't changed. Just the context.

At its core, persistence is about converting failure into feedback. Instead of viewing setbacks as terminal roadblocks, persistent professionals treat them as temporary detours—each one a lesson in disguise. By reframing failure as fuel for adaptation and improvement, we build not only resilience, but also the innovative thinking that drives real growth. True progress often comes after a series of learned experiences that didn't look like success at the time.

Your delta is the distance between where you start and how far you're willing to go.

When I played college football, my skills were far below average—but I showed up anyway. Every day, every rep, every setback was a chance to close the gap. I didn't become the best. I became someone who never stopped closing the distance.

Later in life, when my "basement" was higher—in sales, business, leadership—I applied that same attitude. That's when things really took off. The delta stayed with me.

If you're starting from the bottom, good. That just means your delta is bigger—and so is your opportunity to grow.

Transferring energy to a new purpose is another crucial aspect of persistence, especially when pathways appear blocked. This guideline suggests that when facing immovable obstacles, redirecting focus and efforts toward a fresh endeavor can be incredibly rewarding. For instance, many successful entrepreneurs started with one idea that didn't pan out, only to pivot and channel their determination into a different project that ultimately thrived. By allowing oneself the flexibility to explore diverse routes, persistence effectively transforms from mere stubbornness to dynamic adaptability, embracing change while staying committed to overarching goals.

Furthermore, persistence is closely tied to curiosity and the willingness to question existing norms. The drive to keep challenging the status quo fosters creativity and innovation. Persistent professionals constantly ask, "What if?" and "Why not?" paving the way for groundbreaking ideas and solutions. It's this unyielding spirit of inquiry that keeps the competitive edge sharp and propels industries forward.

Enjoying the moment and staying present embodies another guideline that enhances persistence by reducing burnout and boosting mental well-being. While it may sound counterintuitive, taking time to savor small achievements along the journey can fuel long-term perseverance. Celebrating these moments reinforces motivation, serving as reminders of how far one has come, even amid ongoing challenges. In pressured fields, balancing focus on current tasks with acknowledgment of past milestones cultivates gratitude and fuels the continuous drive needed to tackle future obstacles head-on.

Balance between persistence and presence ensures sustained performance without falling into the trap of relentless hustle culture. Persistent individuals understand when to push forward and when to pause, reflect, and recharge. This balance allows for clearer thinking, sharper decision-making, and, ultimately, more innovative results.

Over time, persistence reveals itself not as a singular effort, but a continuous journey marked by flexibility, resilience, and the courage to innovate. In a world teeming with competition and rapid change, the ability to persistently transform challenges into opportunities distinguishes those who excel from those who remain stagnant. By turning setbacks into lessons, redirecting energy with intention, and celebrating progress along the way, you build the kind of resilience that doesn't just endure—it evolves and helps evolve the environments you move through.

Being Present and Avoiding Extremes

Not all environments are external. The spaces we create in our minds—the energy we allow in, the stories we tell ourselves—matter just as much as the offices we sit in or the people we surround ourselves with.

Take it from a guy who once lived like the movie *San Andreas*.

You know the kind of film I'm talking about—where the world keeps falling apart, one disaster after another, barely a breath between calamities. At one point I was watching that movie and realized something: *This is how most people live*. One crisis ends, another begins. We're addicted to chaos, trained to expect it, even seek it out. And like in the movie, we never pause long enough to actually learn from what just happened.

Have you ever watched certain movies and felt completely exhausted afterward—not physically, but emotionally? Some films have such an interfering energetic impact that it leaves you drained. It's not just about watching characters make decisions; it's the emotional roller coaster that pulls you in, scene after scene, with no time to breathe.

And the truth is, if that's the emotional environment you're living in—whether at work or at home—it's going to cost you. It's going to interfere with your potential. It's going to burn you out. And you might not even realize it's happening, because it's become normal. But just because it's common doesn't mean it's healthy.

Don't build your life like *San Andreas*. Don't make your

environment one long chain reaction of emotional reactivity. Instead, start building a different kind of environment—one rooted in awareness, recovery, and direction. One where you use energy instead of being used by it.

That's where mindfulness comes in.

Mindfulness isn't just about meditation or breathing techniques. It's about how you relate to your environment—internally and externally. It's about your ability to stay grounded in the middle of pressure. To notice what's happening inside you while everything around you is demanding a reaction. To pause long enough to choose a response rather than default to a reflex.

We often talk about creating the right physical environments—an office that reflects your values, a home that restores you, a team that inspires you. But none of those things can function well if your internal environment is in chaos. If you're constantly in emotional reaction mode, no amount of external order will give you peace.

That's why being present matters. Not because it's trendy or spiritual, but because it's practical. In high-pressure industries—sales, entrepreneurship, media, management—people are praised for being relentless. But relentless without recovery is just self-destruction in slow motion.

Mindfulness allows you to be relentless with rhythm. It helps you create internal space so that you can operate in high-stakes environments without letting them shape your identity or hijack your energy. It's about shortening the distance between impact and clarity—between the moment something hard happens and your ability to respond with intention.

Think about the kind of environments you're creating with your energy. Are you building a space that supports calm, clarity, and contribution? Or one that feeds urgency, chaos, and ego?

Ego, by the way, is a major disrupter of healthy environments. I've said before, it stands for *Edging Goodness Out*. When ego is driving your decisions, you stop building environments that are good for you—and start building ones that make you look good. You stay late not because you love the work, but because you want to be seen staying late. You overload your schedule with commitments that don't align with your values because your ego needs to prove something.

But when you're grounded, when you're mindful, you start making different choices. You walk into the same office, but your experience changes. You interact with the same people, but your reactions soften. You leave room to breathe—and that room becomes the space where better relationships, better ideas, and better decisions grow.

Mindfulness creates a filter. It helps you screen what you let in and what you send out. And when you live with that kind of awareness, you start to transform your environments from the inside out. You build places that sustain you instead of drain you. That's what the right environment really is: not a perfect setting, but one that supports who you're trying to become.

So ask yourself: Is the life you're building designed with intention? Or are you just reacting to the next emotional earthquake?

If you want to attract peace, you have to practice it. If you want to live in a space that helps you grow, you have to stop feeding the drama. And if you want to get where you're going—especially in fast-moving industries—you have to stop living like *San Andreas*, and start building like someone who believes ease, clarity, and recovery are not luxuries, but leadership tools.

The most successful people I know don't live in extremes. They live in rhythm. They protect their peace the way others protect their passwords. They know that rest is not a reward—it's a requirement.

And they aren't afraid to redesign their surroundings—mental and physical—until it supports that truth.

Creating Positive Energy

The atmosphere you create isn't just about mood; it's a powerful force that influences interactions and relationships.

Imagine walking into a room where tension is palpable; conversations are stilted, your body feels heavy, and stress looms. Now, picture entering a space filled with warmth and positivity—a relaxed atmosphere where ideas flow freely, and collaboration is instinctive. This difference is often rooted in the energy generated by those present, proving that attitudes shape environments as much as physical settings do.

The power of positive energy lies in its ripple effect. By infusing spaces with optimism, calmness, and empathy, you become a beacon of trust and support. Consider a scenario where a manager handles high-pressure situations with understanding. Their approach not only eases tensions but encourages open communication and fosters a sense of security among team members. In doing so, diverse ideas blossom, inspiration thrives, and collective progress becomes attainable.

This kind of environment is especially important when interacting with children. They are remarkably perceptive and absorb the energy surrounding them more keenly than adults. When met with frustration or negativity, they may build walls to protect themselves, hindering potential growth and learning. However, when greeted with patience and encouragement, children flourish. They learn to approach problems creatively, develop resilience, and foster healthy social skills, all foundational for future success.

Setting a positive example extends beyond professional circles and familial ties—it permeates public spheres, influencing casual acquaintances and strangers alike. Think about an experience of witnessing someone being kind to a stranger in distress; it uplifts not only the involved parties but inspires onlookers to act similarly. This contagious nature of a benevolent spirit highlights why embodying these traits consistently reinforces communal harmony and shared happiness.

Creating such environments doesn't require grand gestures. It begins with small, intentional actions: listening actively, offering help without expecting returns, or simply smiling more often. Over time, these behaviors compound, transforming workplaces and communities into places characterized by mutual respect and productivity.

For professionals in dynamic fields, where stress levels are inherently high, maintaining equilibrium and exuding positivity is vital. It serves as a reminder that, despite challenges, there's strength in unity, and achievements are amplified through collaboration.

To effectively set an exemplary example, consider incorporating structured approaches. Develop habits that align with nurturing these qualities—whether through mindfulness practices, prioritizing work-life balance, or engaging in activities that promote mental well-being. The deliberate cultivation of a positive mindset ensures that it remains genuine rather than forced, making it more impactful.

By nurturing such an environment, you're not only paving the way for your growth but also enabling others' development. Those around you tend to mirror positive behaviors, creating a feedback loop that continually enriches experiences within that space.

In competitive sectors like advertising or management, this approach enhances creativity and innovation. Teams unite over shared goals, fostering an atmosphere where all feel valued and empowered to contribute meaningfully. Consequently, projects advance smoothly, client relations improve, and organizational objectives are achieved more efficiently.

Furthermore, in sports and entertainment, where teamwork and synergy are paramount, instilling positive energy becomes even more crucial. Athletes, actors, and performers thrive when backed by supportive peers and constructive environments. It boosts morale, aids focus, and enhances performance, ultimately contributing to both individual accolades and team victories.

Reflecting on media and journalism, where information is constantly flowing, creating a positive environment helps maintain integrity and objectivity. Journalists working under stress can inadvertently let biases slip, whereas those operating in a supportive network are better positioned to deliver accurate, balanced stories that inform and educate the public effectively.

Your Environment on Your Time

Imagine a day where your calendar seamlessly integrates meetings, deadlines, family dinners, and personal downtime. By scheduling personal and family time alongside work commitments, you establish a foundation of balance. This deliberate planning ensures that important moments with loved ones are not overshadowed by professional pursuits. It allows you to be present at family gatherings or enjoy a hobby without the lingering stress of pending work tasks.

A systematic approach to scheduling also helps prevent conflicts that can arise in both personal and professional spheres. When personal appointments collide with work commitments, stress levels rise, impacting performance and relationships. On the other hand, a well-structured schedule acts as a buffer, reducing potential overlaps and easing pressure. This foresight fosters a peaceful environment where both spheres of life can thrive independently yet harmoniously.

Consistency is key to maintaining this equilibrium. Regularly updating and adhering to a schedule reinforces boundaries between work and personal life. Over time, this practice encourages the development of routines that promote stability and predictability. These routines, once established, become second nature, eliminating unnecessary decision-making processes and freeing mental space for more productive endeavors.

This structured approach is not about rigid control but about making space for spontaneity within a framework. By having a clear plan for when work ends and personal time begins, you create the freedom to be flexible within those defined hours. For instance, knowing that your evenings are reserved for personal activities allows you to embrace impromptu dinner plans or enjoy a quiet night in with your favorite book or movie.

Achieving happiness through structured time management requires intentional decisions and prioritization of what truly matters. It's about choosing to invest time in activities and relationships that align with your values and bring joy and fulfillment. This choice often means saying no to tasks or obligations that do not serve these goals, a concept that might be difficult initially but becomes easier with practice.

To illustrate, consider an entrepreneur who balances their start-up's demands with family life. By dedicating specific times each week for family dinners or weekend outings, they ensure that their presence is felt both at home and in the business. This intentional separation of roles not only enhances their quality of life but also sets a positive example for their team, promoting a culture of respect for personal boundaries.

Moreover, structured time management encourages reflection and assessment of tasks performed throughout the day. It allows you to evaluate where time was well spent and where adjustments might be necessary. This ongoing process of refinement leads to more effective use of time and increased productivity.

The journey toward better time management is not without challenges. Procrastination, unexpected emergencies, and shifting priorities can disrupt even the best-laid plans. However, approaching time with a flexible mindset and readiness to adapt allows for resilience in the face of such disruptions.

It's vital to remember that the goal is progress, not perfection.

Being mindful of how we manage our time reflects understanding its finite nature. Each moment invested wisely contributes to overall life satisfaction. In essence, incorporating structured time management into our daily routines empowers us to live intentionally, ensuring that our professional success does not come at the expense of our personal well-being.

Final Insights

In this chapter, we explored how the environments we choose—both external and internal—shape the trajectory of our growth. Whether it's your physical workspace, the people around you, or the emotional patterns you live inside of, your environment is either supporting your evolution or silently sabotaging it.

And here's the truth: Not all environments are visible. Think about that awful environment I was inviting into my life when I was the dick with the Ferrari. Some of the most important spaces we live in are internal—our thoughts, reactions, stories, and energy patterns. As we saw in the *San Andreas* story, living in constant emotional reactivity can become its own exhausting environment. But when we begin to build from a place of intention and mindfulness, everything changes. We become the architects of calmer, more creative, more aligned spaces—within and around us.

True alignment between your values and your environment doesn't just reduce stress—it unlocks momentum. You start to operate from flow instead of force. From clarity instead of chaos.

And that's where transformation really begins.

Guidelines

- Know your delta. Let your bottom be a springboard for growth, not a weakness.
- Treat your internal state like a space you're curating. Is it cluttered or clear?
- Make mindfulness a maintenance tool—not a luxury.
- Choose recovery over reactivity.
- Structure your day so that energy is protected, not drained.
- Lead with presence, not pressure.

Takeaways

- Right environments don't just look good—they feel right.
- You're not just living in spaces; you're building them, moment by moment.

- Energy is contagious—yours and everyone else's. Be intentional about what you absorb and project.
- A calm internal space makes it easier to thrive in chaotic external ones.
- Ease isn't weakness. It's strategy.

Ask Yourself

- Is my workspace aligned with my personal values and goals—or is it draining me?
- Am I surrounding myself with places that elevate me?
- What part of my environment could I optimize to feel more energized, creative, and in flow?

Your environment should feel like fuel, not friction. Whether it's a physical space, a mental story, or an emotional cycle—design it with intention. Because when your surroundings are aligned with who you are and where you're going, you don't just survive. You thrive. Here's a simple framework to help you assess whether your surroundings are helping or hurting:

- **Audit the Energy:** After a workday, do you feel expanded or depleted? If your environment doesn't elevate your spirit, it's time to recalibrate.
- **Spot the Disconnects:** If you're forcing productivity in stale or toxic spaces, pause. Disconnection from purpose often shows up as burnout, resistance, or lack of creativity.
- **Align Passion with Place:** Environment isn't just physical—it's energetic. Create sacred time blocks, rejuvenating spaces, and moments of stillness to stay in the flow.

So much of this chapter has been about learning to live differently—less like *San Andreas*, more like someone building with purpose. That movie wasn't just entertainment—it was a mirror. A warning. When you live in constant reactivity, when your environment becomes one emotional earthquake after another, you don't grow—you brace. But when you pause, breathe, and choose where you stand and how you respond, you stop surviving the chaos and start creating calm. The real power isn't in avoiding disasters—it's in learning to build steady ground inside them. There's no shame in driving a Chevy Volt . . . or parking it legally.

Chapter 3

THINK WITH YOUR BRAIN HEAD, NOT YOUR DICK HEAD

Surround Yourself with the Right Thinking

Throughout my life, I've learned that the quality of your thoughts directly shapes the quality of your life. Ideas aren't just things we think—they're environments we live inside of. And just like people or places, the wrong ideas can drag you down, while the right ones can lift you up.

When I was in law school, I had a big sister named Kim Theriault. She took care of me, and years later, when she graduated and became a federal judge, she invited me to her graduation party. Kim was a true Cajun, born in Thibodaux, Louisiana, and I'd never been deep into Cajun country before. So I drove out past New Orleans to join the celebration—crawfish ponds, deep fryers, three homes on the land, and more joy and unity than I'd seen in a long time.

But the best part of the trip? Meeting her grandfather—Grandpa No Way. He was nearly 100 years old, sitting under a tree with a cold beer in one hand, a cigarette in the other, and a plate of catfish with hot sauce in front of him. Naturally, I sat down to ask him about life. I love talking to people near 100—it's like unlocking secrets.

I asked him how he got his name.

He said, "Well, when I was born, I weighed twelve pounds, six ounces. The doctor took one look at me and said, 'No way.' So my mom said, 'That's his name.'"

But what he said next has stayed with me ever since.

"I've lived my whole life with an attitude of 'No way I can't do it.' When someone tells me I can't, I just say, 'No way.' You want to live a long life? Be happy. That's the most valuable practice I have."

That moment taught me one of the most powerful lessons I've ever learned: Mindset is everything. It doesn't matter how unconventional your habits are or where you come from. If your thoughts are rooted in belief and joy, they will carry you.

In this chapter, we explore the power of that mindset—of surrounding yourself with ideas that fuel clarity, confidence, and momentum. We'll look at how the media you consume, the conversations you engage in, and even the background noise in your life shapes your thoughts—and how your thoughts shape your outcomes. Whether you're building a business, leading a team, or just trying to stay sane in a high-pressure world, this chapter will help you curate the right ideas so your mind becomes a place of power, not self-sabotage.

The Power of Ideas in Our Surroundings

Be happy.

That was Grandpa No Way's big pitch.

It was a simple idea with all the power in the world because the ideas we allow into our minds can have profound effects on our thoughts and actions. Our thoughts operate at high speeds, shaping not only how we see the world but also how we react to it. Imagine our minds as complex networks where every thought is a spark traveling through a web of connections. Each spark holds the potential to shift our entire mindset. To truly harness the power of these influences, it is essential to consciously choose the right ideas that resonate with positive vibrations.

Thoughts, much like radio waves, vibrate at different frequencies. Some carry positivity, filling us with energy and enthusiasm, while others may drag us down, making tasks feel arduous. These high-speed vibrations affect our perceptions, which in turn influence our actions. For instance, if you wake up thinking today will be a productive day, this thought sets a tone for your actions, encouraging you to tackle tasks with vigor. Conversely, doubting your abilities first thing in the morning might slow you down before you even start.

The source of these thoughts often lies in the ideas that surround us. Ideas are absorbed through various channels: conversations with colleagues, news channels on our commute, or the podcasts we listen to during workouts. Over time, repeated exposure to certain ideas ingrains them into our belief systems, sometimes so subtly we hardly notice. Consider the example of a sales professional who consistently hears negative projections about market trends. Such persistent exposure may seep into their perception, affecting confidence and decision-making processes. On the flip side, surrounding oneself with successful role models in sales meetings or motivational talks can nurture an optimistic outlook, reshaping beliefs around what's achievable.

Audio input plays a crucial role here. The sounds we regularly encounter contribute to creating mental chemistries that either boost or hinder us. Positive sounds, like uplifting music or encouraging dialogue, can produce beneficial mental chemistry, enhancing creativity and problem-solving skills. This concept finds backing in research, suggesting that music tuned to particular frequencies can stimulate stress relief and improved concentration. Imagine sitting at your desk, overwhelmed by deadlines, and choosing to play a calm and rhythmic tune. Almost magically, the tension dissipates, replaced by clarity and focus—a testament to the power of sound.

But it's not just music or spoken words; even ambient noise contributes. Consider the difference between working in a chaotic, noisy environment and one filled with serene background sounds like gentle rain or soft instrumentals. The latter creates an atmosphere conducive to productive thought, reflecting in the quality of the work produced. Marketing professionals often leverage this understanding, curating office playlists designed to foster creativity and a collaborative spirit among teams.

However, the relationship between ideas, perceptions, and actions is not linear but rather a continuous feedback loop. When actions informed by positive perceptions lead to success, they reinforce the initial positive thoughts, strengthening the whole cycle. For example, an advertiser who believes in groundbreaking campaigns may push boundaries, resulting in innovative work that receives accolades. This reward reinforces their belief system, prompting further creative endeavors.

To capitalize on this loop, it is important to mindfully choose the content we consume daily. Reading uplifting articles, engaging in constructive discussions, or listening to inspiring speeches can fill our minds with productive ideas. Likewise, analyzing success stories from known figures in management or entertainment can instill hopeful perspectives, encouraging us to emulate such accomplishments.

In professional settings, team leaders can cultivate this mindset by incorporating daily briefings featuring positive insights or celebrating small wins, thus embedding the right vibrations into the team's routine. Frequent exposure to positive reiterations transforms skepticism into belief, energizing individuals to pursue excellence with unwavering determination.

Communicating with Awareness

I'll never forget the time I lost a deal—not because I lacked the right pitch, but because I didn't listen. I was so busy preparing what I was going to say next that I completely missed what the client was trying to tell me. When I finally stopped talking, the silence on the other end wasn't thoughtful—it was final. They said, "Thanks, but I think we'll pass."

That moment stung. But it also taught me one of the most important lessons in my life and career: Real communication isn't about being the loudest or the smartest voice in the room. It's about being the clearest, calmest, and most present.

To begin with, speaking kindly and practicing graciousness are not mere courtesies but essential elements that significantly contribute to this atmosphere of thoughtfulness. We frequently find ourselves in situations where emotions can flare up easily. I know emotions were short and hot when we were trying to move the Rams from one city to another. In such environments, it's crucial to understand that words once spoken cannot be taken back, and they often leave lasting impressions. Speaking kindly involves choosing our words wisely and ensuring they reflect consideration and respect for others. It is about being mindful and intentional with language, knowing that the words we use can either uplift or discourage colleagues and clients alike. Practicing graciousness daily, therefore, becomes an exercise in resilience and empathy, helping us maintain composure and professionalism even in challenging moments.

However, maintaining this level of thoughtful communication requires more than just intention; it necessitates a set of practical tools that enable us to manage our emotional responses effectively. One powerful technique is deep breathing. Simple yet profound, deep breathing acts as an anchor in turbulent situations. When faced with adversity or stress, taking deliberate, slow breaths can help calm the mind, reduce stress levels, and regain control over our speech. This practice not only aids in centering ourselves but also allows us to respond thoughtfully rather than reacting impulsively. As we incorporate deep breathing into our daily routine, it gradually becomes a natural reflex, equipping us with the grace to handle almost any situation with poise and clarity.

While speaking kindly and using techniques like deep breathing help manage what comes out of our mouths, tuning our minds toward gratitude and empathy plays a crucial role in preventing regretful words from surfacing in the first place. Reengineering our thoughts means consciously shifting our focus to recognize positive aspects in every situation. For instance, when a team meeting doesn't go as planned, instead of dwelling on the negatives, look for achievements or learning opportunities. By cultivating gratitude, we open avenues to appreciate differences, leading to more harmonious communications.

Empathy further deepens this process. By putting ourselves in another person's shoes, we gain insights into their feelings and perspectives, which fosters understanding rather than conflict. Empathy transforms our communication style from self-centered to inclusive and compassionate. This shift not only boosts morale within teams but also paves the way for collaborative success.

Creating an environment where thoughtful communication thrives involves a conscious effort to influence our mental landscape positively. Consider the impact of the media you consume—stay vigilant against negativity that might creep into your mindset without notice. Seek content that uplifts and inspires, as it tends to mirror in your thought patterns, and thus your communication style. Consciously creating positive thoughts isn't just beneficial for personal well-being; it becomes pivotal in shaping our interactions with others. By setting intentions each day to speak kindly, breathe deeply, and reframe thoughts with empathy and gratitude, professionals develop the skills needed to navigate complex social dynamics effectively.

Positive Influences from Media Consumption

One way I'm pretty sure that Grandpa No Way got to almost 100 happy and healthy and surrounded by living family was looking at the television with a bit of skepticism.

The influence of media on our emotions and mindsets is profound, often more significant than we realize. Real or fictional events can evoke powerful emotional responses. We shouldn't look away from the hard things, but we can look toward them with compassion, or with acceptance, or with skepticism, and evaluate what they might mean to us and how they might influence our thinking. Consider how a movie like *San Andreas* captures viewers' imaginations with its spectacular depiction of natural disasters. Despite its fictional premise, the film's portrayal of chaos and survival can leave audiences feeling intense emotions such as fear, excitement, or empathy.

This phenomenon occurs because our brains process visual and auditory stimuli in ways that engage our emotions. When we watch a movie, our minds immerse us in the story, leading us to experience emotions that feel genuine. This effect showcases the media's capacity to influence not just immediate feelings but also long-term attitudes and behaviors. Frequent exposure to specific themes or narratives can subtly shape our beliefs and perceptions.

Understanding these influences becomes crucial when striving for emotional balance in a world where we have very little time to slow down and really take in how what we let in might emotionally impact us. By recognizing how media impacts us, we can make more conscious choices about what content we consume, adapting our media habits to preserve our mental well-being. This awareness allows individuals to manage their emotional responses better, avoiding unnecessary stress or agitation caused by media consumption.

Moreover, remaining aware of these influences can aid professionals in industries like sales, marketing, and entertainment. People working in these fields are often tasked with understanding audience emotions and reactions to craft compelling messages or products.

Awareness of the impact of media helps these professionals design experiences that resonate positively with their audiences.

To maintain control over our emotional landscape, it's essential to witness and receive acts of kindness. Exposure to positive media content, such as uplifting stories or depictions of altruism, can counterbalance the negative emotional impact of more intense fictional works. Embracing generosity within oneself despite others' reactions can be mirrored in choosing media that reinforces positivity and hope.

Practically speaking, one guideline to consider is periodically auditing your media diet. Reflect on how certain films, shows, or news outlets make you feel. Do they energize or drain you? Do they inspire optimism or feed into anxiety? This introspective approach empowers individuals to curate their media interactions thoughtfully, fostering an environment that supports mental resilience.

Staying generous despite others' reactions is another aspect of balancing media influence. In our highly connected world, where social media amplifies both negativity and positivity, maintaining this mindset helps navigate digital spaces while preserving personal peace. Engaging with content that promotes generosity—in both online and offline contexts—can serve as a grounding force amid the cacophony of media noise.

The Practice of Kindness and Generosity

Imagine walking into a room and being greeted with a warm smile, a genuine expression of kindness. Consider how such encounters can change the course of your day, lightening burdens you might not have even been aware you were carrying. This is the transformative power of kindness—a force so simple, yet profound, that can redefine interactions and influence mindsets in remarkable ways. Kindness isn't merely an action but a powerful catalyst for change, weaving connections that enhance our lives both personally and professionally.

To truly comprehend kindness's impact, it must be experienced from multiple perspectives: giving, receiving, and witnessing. Practicing acts of kindness creates ripples that extend beyond the immediate interaction. Imagine helping a colleague struggling with a deadline or offering your seat to someone who needs it more on a crowded train. These small gestures are capable of fostering a culture of support and understanding, promoting a sense of belonging. When we receive kindness, it often surprises us, creating a sense of gratitude that compels us to pass it forward, thus continuing the cycle. Witnessing acts of kindness can be just as powerful, serving as a reminder that empathy and generosity still exist in a world that sometimes seems indifferent. It's these moments that can inspire us to emulate the goodness we've observed, enriching our environments.

Generosity is deeply rooted within us; it's a natural extension of our intrinsic values and beliefs. We cannot recognize true generosity in others if we don't first cultivate it within ourselves. Holding on to anger or resentment can cloud our perception, making it difficult to appreciate the beauty in altruistic actions. For instance, consider an athlete who constantly competes with a mindset of scarcity, convinced that their success hinges on the failure of others. Compare this with another who cheers for their teammates' achievements, sharing insights and encouragement openly. The generous athlete likely experiences more fulfillment and joy because they have embraced abundance over limitation.

To nurture this inner generosity, one must embrace positivity and self-reflection, peeling back layers of preconceived notions and biases that hinder personal growth. Engaging in practices like journaling or meditation can help unveil the subtleties of your internal landscape, revealing areas where you can practice greater kindness toward yourself and others. Kindness and generosity aren't attributes that appear overnight; they require continuous nurturing and dedication. Only by cultivating this internal compassion can it seamlessly manifest outward, impacting those we encounter daily.

Creating a positive internal environment impacts not only your personal well-being but also how you engage with the world around you. Picture your mind as a garden, where the seeds you plant determine what will flourish. If negativity and mistrust are sown, the resulting harvest will likely mirror these traits. Conversely, sowing seeds of kindness and integrity will yield a bounty of respect, honesty, and connection. A positive internal environment serves as fertile ground for kindness to blossom beautifully, touching every aspect of your life.

For professionals, especially those navigating high-pressure environments, maintaining this positivity can be challenging. It's crucial to infuse workspaces with elements that reinforce kindness and trust—be it through open communication channels, team-building activities, or mentorship programs. Managers, for instance, wield significant influence over workplace culture. By leading with empathy and fairness, they can model the behavior they wish to see, encouraging teams to adopt a similar approach. In turn, this environment fosters collaboration and innovation, as individuals feel valued and empowered to contribute without fear of judgment.

The ripple effect of a positive internal environment extends beyond the individual, influencing broader organizational dynamics and societal structures. Communities built on mutual respect and understanding are more resilient, thriving in the face of adversity. They serve as havens where creativity is celebrated, mistakes are seen as learning opportunities, and everyone's voice holds value.

Transformative change is possible when each person commits to nurturing their inner kindness, thereby amplifying its impact externally.

Harnessing Positive Thoughts for Creation

Our thoughts hold a unique power—both in our work lives and our personal lives. They are more than mere reflections; they are the guiding forces that shape our emotions and drive our actions. Our thoughts can feel like whispers in the chaos, wielding an influence that ultimately can lead to happiness or descend into darker realms of depression. As such, understanding and harnessing this power is central to crafting a life filled with positivity and purpose.

Imagine your brain as the most valuable asset you have—it truly is. Every thought we entertain can either build us up or break us down. When you're immersed in professional fields like sales, marketing, or entrepreneurship, this becomes even clearer. The thoughts we nurture become the framework upon which we build our dreams and actions. If these thoughts are aligned positively, they serve as beacons, lighting the way to new opportunities and memorable experiences.

Positive visualization plays a fundamental role in this mental process. It's akin to setting the GPS of your mind toward destinations of success and contentment. Picture yourself at the pinnacle of your career or in a personal achievement—this isn't just daydreaming. Visualizing success has been shown to open doors we might not have noticed otherwise. It creates a mental map that guides our actions and decisions, leading us toward paths that align with our goals. For instance, athletes often use positive visualization to enhance performance. By mentally rehearsing their best game, they prime their minds for real-time achievements. This practice can easily translate to any profession or personal endeavor.

Moreover, positive visualization isn't merely about achieving grand successes. It's about creating moments of joy and significance in everyday life. Consider a moment when you visualized an important meeting going well, and it did, or when you imagined a family gathering filled with laughter, which turned out exactly as hoped. These special memories, often sparked by simple acts of visualization, enrich our lives profoundly.

The transformative power of a single empowering thought cannot be overstated. It's often the catalyst for significant change—a spark that ignites a chain reaction of positive events and outcomes. Think of historical leaders or innovators throughout time who initiated monumental shifts in society, driven by the power of a single liberating idea. Such a thought can offer clarity amid confusion, a steady course in uncertain waters, or the courage to pursue new ventures.

We can draw from examples found all around us. Take, for instance, entrepreneurs who transformed industry norms with one bold idea. Their mental landscapes were no different from ours; they simply learned to channel their thinking productively. This empowerment begins with recognizing the potent influence our thoughts have over our realities.

Here's a guideline inspired by Grandpa No Way that highlights the importance of keeping laughter and positivity at the forefront of thinking. Laughter, after all, is a universal language of joy. Embracing positivity, much like laughter, invites warmth into our interactions and inner dialogues. Encourage yourself to find humor in daily frustrations or connect with others through shared jokes—these small acts contribute to an uplifting mindset. It's essential to approach life with a sense of lightness, reminding ourselves that many stresses are temporary and surmountable.

Taking control of our thought processes is not an easy task. It requires conscious effort, dedication, and sometimes, reprogramming of patterns ingrained within us. Yet, the rewards are immeasurable. With each conscious choice to nurture a positive thought, visualize a desired outcome, or embrace empowering beliefs, we create ripples that spread through every aspect of our lives. These ripples extend into our professional circles, influencing how we interact, react, and make decisions.

Consider starting each day with a moment of reflection where you set an intention grounded in positivity. Whether facing a challenging project, preparing for a crucial presentation, or navigating complex interpersonal dynamics, drawing strength from a foundation of positive thinking helps mediate stress and anxiety. It allows you to approach situations with composure and confidence. Remember, every thought counts, and choosing wisely among them shapes the trajectory of our journey.

Final Insights

Our journey through this chapter has explored the profound impact that surrounding ourselves with the right ideas can have on our thoughts and actions. We've delved into how these positive influences resonate within us, shaping not only the way we perceive the world but also how we choose to engage with it. By consciously selecting what we let into our minds—whether through the words we hear, the media we consume, or the ambient sounds in our environment—we nurture a mental landscape that fosters growth and optimism. It's about creating an ecosystem where positivity thrives, resulting in vibrant thoughts that energize and propel us forward in our personal and professional lives.

From Grandpa No Way's legendary attitude, to the professional ripple effects of media, sound, and spoken word, we've seen how the right ideas can powerfully shape behavior, creativity, and resilience. Your thoughts don't just react to your environment—they create it.

Whether it's tuning your mental dial to more positive frequencies, reengineering communication through empathy, or setting a tone of kindness and generosity in every interaction, your mindset acts as a filter for your reality. Thoughtfulness isn't just a personal virtue—it's a strategic advantage. The stories you tell yourself, and the stories you listen to, shape what you believe is possible.

When you think with intention, your actions begin to align. And when your actions align, your environment begins to change—from pressure to possibility.

Guidelines

- Start your day by setting the tone—ask yourself, "What do I want to think with today?"
- Pause before speaking—use deep breathing to regulate emotion and foster clarity.
- Curate your content diet—read, watch, and listen to media that uplifts and inspires.
- Look for gratitude in your reactions—especially when things don't go your way.
- Practice kindness as an energy tool, not just a social gesture.
- Visualize your desired outcomes and trace them back to empowering beliefs.

Takeaways

- Thoughts are environments—you live inside the ones you nurture.
- A single empowering idea can shift your entire trajectory.
- Empathy and clarity beat volume and ego every time.
- Positive energy isn't luck—it's engineered through habits and awareness.
- Grandpa No Way was right—attitude is longevity.

Ask Yourself

- What's one idea I'm holding on to that no longer serves me?
- How might I communicate more clearly, more calmly, or more kindly today?
- Is my inner voice fueling growth—or feeding self-doubt?
- What media or inputs do I need to limit or replace to protect my mental clarity?

As we conclude, let's emphasize the continuous loop of positivity. And let's move forward thinking with our brain heads—not our dick heads. The actions inspired by nurturing surroundings reinforce our beliefs, which then translate into successful outcomes, further fueling a cycle of inspiration and achievement. Ultimately, the right ideas and right thinking act as guiding lights, illuminating paths toward fulfillment and success for all who venture down them.

You are not powerless against the noise. You can choose your inputs. You can reframe your thoughts. And you can build an internal environment rooted in clarity, connection, and contribution.

Because when someone tells you "No way," you can choose to hear it the way Grandpa No Way did—not as a limit, but as a challenge. A spark. A mindset. One that says, without hesitation: "No way I can't."

Chapter 4

DON'T SERVICE A DICK

Surround Yourself with the Right Service

When we talk about acts and actions of right service, we often picture people like first responders, veterans, teachers—and, of course, our moms. I was lucky enough to be raised by one of the most selfless people I've ever known: my mother. She didn't just teach me about service—she lived it.

She worked two jobs. During the day, she was a second-grade teacher making $17,000 a year. At night, she'd pack us dinner in a paper bag and drive around Akron, Ohio, refilling turnstiles with greeting cards just so we could get by. She once used our food stamps to buy pencils for the kids in her class. That's the kind of woman she was.

She raised a family, taught Sunday school, led in her community, and fought for women's rights—even though, at the time, she couldn't even get a credit card in her own name without a man to cosign. She served without recognition or reward. Because that's what true service looks like: showing up, even when no one's watching.

When you surround yourself with a devotion to right service, you surround yourself with people who serve others because it's who they are—not because they expect anything in return.

Now, receiving that kind of service? That's a whole other challenge.

Prioritizing self-care and meaningful service is a matter of recognizing the delicate balance between looking after yourself and making impactful contributions to your community. In our often chaotic world, it's crucial to understand that taking care of your own needs doesn't only benefit you; it enhances your capacity to help others as well. Imagine navigating a career in sales or marketing, where demands are high, yet energy can easily deplete without proper attention to personal wellness. The key lies in avoiding burnout by ensuring that your own reserves are full before extending assistance to those around you.

This chapter will unravel the powerful synergy created when personal well-being aligns with purposeful service. You will explore how self-care is not an act of selfishness, but rather a strategy for sustainability, allowing you to effectively contribute to your professional and personal circles. Through examples spanning various fields—sales, entrepreneurship, sports, and media—you'll gain insights into establishing boundaries and finding fulfillment. By understanding the connection between looking after yourself and uplifting others, you'll discover ways to foster both personal success and shared prosperity without falling into the trap of serving just for the sake of it.

Stay Visible, Stay Well, Stay Connected

My mom taught me everything I know about service—but not so much about self-care. Like a lot of people raised to give, she poured herself into others so fully that she rarely made room for herself. She raised us on food stamps, worked two jobs, taught Sunday school, led on women's rights, and still found time to pack our dinners and fill greeting card turnstiles across Akron. That was her normal. But looking back, I realize she rarely gave herself the same care she gave everyone else. As a kid, I thought that was normal. As an adult, I realized: You can't serve others well if you're running on empty.

And she's not alone.

So many of us are taught to give relentlessly—but rarely taught how to *receive*, let alone how to *replenish*. We think service means sacrifice. But the truth is, the best service is sustainable. It's grounded in energy that's been protected and restored, not drained and stretched thin. I know I've spent times in my life running myself into the ground trying to please clients, hit targets, or prove my worth. But when you serve from depletion, your impact diminishes. You lose clarity, empathy, creativity—and eventually, your capacity to serve at all.

Self-care isn't selfish. It's strategic. It's what allows you to serve longer, love harder, lead better. Whether it's through small moments of stillness, intentional boundaries, or asking for help when you need it, protecting your well-being becomes the foundation of your contribution to others.

Think of the people in your life who make the greatest impact—first responders, teachers, parents, veterans. The ones who last are the ones who know how to rest, reset, and refuel. The ones who know that service is not about martyrdom—it's about momentum. And you can't keep momentum if your tank is empty.

The people who serve best aren't the ones who give until they disappear. They're the ones who stay visible, stay well, and stay connected to why they started in the first place.

That's what this section is about—not self-care as spa days or bubble baths, but as a strategy for sustainable service. The best service isn't the loudest or the most visible. It's the kind that lasts.

Self-Interest Versus Selflessness

Balancing self-care with societal contribution—it's a tricky balancing act that hinges on understanding the distinction between constructive self-interest and selflessness.

Constructive self-interest refers to actions that fulfill personal needs while simultaneously offering benefits to the broader community. For instance, when individuals focus on personal development or career advancement, they not only improve their quality of life but also bolster the productivity and innovation within their workplaces. It is vital for professionals to recognize that prioritizing their well-being can lead directly to increased efficiency and creativity, thus contributing more effectively to organizational goals and societal progress.

On a larger scale, wealthy individuals often illustrate this principle through philanthropy and investments that provide substantial benefits to society. Their resources enable them to support educational programs, health initiatives, and community development projects. These contributions may stem from their pursuit of a legacy or personal fulfillment, yet they have profound impacts on collective well-being. Such actions demonstrate how personal gains, when channeled constructively, can generate significant positive outcomes for others.

However, it's important to note that impactful contributions are not solely reserved for those with vast wealth or influence.

Small-scale individual efforts also play a crucial role in fostering communal growth. Consider the volunteer who dedicates weekends to local charities or the mentor who offers guidance to newcomers in the field. While these contributions might seem minor in comparison to large philanthropic endeavors, their cumulative effect over time can create meaningful change. These acts of service reflect an understanding that every effort, regardless of scale, contributes to the social fabric.

Acknowledging healthy self-interest as a driving force aligns with the notion of communal growth. When individuals pursue personal interests passionately and responsibly, they often inspire others to do the same. Imagine a salesperson who excels not only by meeting targets but also by innovating new sales strategies. By focusing on their personal success, they inadvertently elevate team performance and, by extension, the company's standing in the industry. Such scenarios underscore how individual pursuits dovetail with shared aspirations, creating a symbiotic relationship where both the individual and community thrive.

The interplay between self-interest and selflessness becomes even clearer when examining the ripple effects of personal achievements. A marketer who invests in self-education to stay current with trends enhances their ability to develop campaigns that resonate more deeply with audiences. Consequently, these improved campaigns lead to better customer engagement and potentially greater business success, which ultimately supports economic stability and growth. Thus, taking steps toward personal enhancement serves not just the individual but fortifies the community.

To gain a deeper appreciation of this dynamic, it's crucial to foster a mindset oriented toward self-discovery rather than comparison. By focusing on personal strengths and areas for growth, professionals can identify unique opportunities to contribute meaningfully without getting trapped in the cycle of measuring oneself against others. This shift in perspective allows for a more authentic form of self-expression and service, where individuals give their best because they choose to, not because they feel compelled to outdo someone else.

Additionally, embracing solitude can be instrumental in refining your sense of purpose and direction. Learning to be comfortable alone equips individuals with the clarity necessary for making decisions that honor both their personal well-being and their responsibilities to others. In a world that often idolizes constant connection and busyness, understanding the value of quiet reflection can lead to more thoughtful and impactful actions.

Ultimately, distinguishing between self-interest and selflessness requires ongoing reflection and a willingness to reassess priorities. Those in competitive fields must regularly evaluate whether their pursuits align with their values and the greater good. In doing so, they cultivate an environment where personal achievements contribute positively to the community, reinforcing the belief that individual growth need not come at the expense of collective welfare.

Fear of Solitude and FOMO

In the high-speed whirlwind of today's professional world, especially in fields like sales, marketing, and entertainment, it's easy to lose yourself in the incessant demands of work and social obligations. One significant fear that often arises is being alone, which can push individuals to constantly seek out social interactions, sometimes to their own detriment. This fear is not uncommon, particularly when the allure of busy gatherings or the persistent hum of constant digital connection feels safer than solitude. Yet, this very avoidance of being alone can lead to neglecting oneself, as personal well-being becomes overshadowed by external engagements.

Consider the scenario where someone habitually fills every moment with social activities, fearing that slowing down might mean missing out on important opportunities or connections. This perpetual busyness often masks an underlying anxiety about solitude, a fear rooted in misunderstanding its true potential. Instead of embracing the quiet moments for reflection and growth, many are swept into a cycle of continuous interaction, driven by the belief that staying plugged in equates to maximizing life's offerings.

The modern phenomenon known as FOMO, or Fear of Missing Out, intensifies this yearning for validation through external means. Every event skipped feels like a lost opportunity for acceptance or validation, pushing individuals to prioritize societal affirmation over personal exploration. When your calendar is dictated by a need for approval, it leaves little room for the introspection necessary for genuine self-discovery. Essentially, FOMO diverts attention away from the rich terrain within—missing the chance to cultivate personal interests or explore uncharted facets of oneself.

Moreover, the pervasive pressure to conform plays a formidable role in distracting from authentic fulfillment. In environments heavy with expectation, such as corporate offices or performance stages, there's an inherent urge to blend in, to meet established standards rather than carve individual paths. This inclination to fit in can stifle unique talents or passions, leading to an inauthentic version of success that doesn't truly resonate with your core values. Over time, this can lead to dissatisfaction and a sense of emptiness, even amid outward achievements.

However, if these fears are faced head-on, there lies an incredible opportunity: solitude. Embracing moments of aloneness doesn't signify loneliness; rather, it's a chance to engage deeply with our thoughts, dreams, and aspirations without the noise of the outside world dictating terms. Solitude allows the mind to wander freely, reaching new insights and ideas that may remain hidden amid constant social input. It becomes a sanctuary where one can recharge, reflect, and gain clarity on what truly brings joy and purpose.

Solitude also offers space for peace—a break from the relentless pursuit of acceptance and conformity. It's where authenticity blossoms, unencumbered by societal expectations. By finding comfort in our company, our confidence and self-assurance strengthens. This lets us return to larger group settings with a refreshed perspective and newfound resilience. Those who lean into solitude often discover a deeper understanding of self, leading to more meaningful contributions both personally and professionally.

Creating abundance by servicing oneself and sharing it is crucial. This means taking the fruits of solitary reflection—whether it's innovative ideas or a revitalized spirit—and using them to enhance both personal and communal experiences. The act of turning inward and then extending outward creates a ripple effect, enriching not just the individual but also the environments they are part of. Here, the guideline of transforming internal abundance into shared benefit becomes essential.

When we meet our own needs, I've found that unconditional service through selfless actions emerges naturally. When self-service isn't neglected, the energy and resources necessary for genuine altruism become available. This wasn't born from obligation but out of a sincere desire to contribute positively, fueled by an inner reservoir of contentment and balance.

The Unsustainable Pursuit of Pleasing Others

It can be all too easy to fall into the habit of trying to please everyone. Yet, this relentless pursuit to cater to others drains your energy and resources, leaving little for yourself. The constant demands placed on professionals can result in burnout, where the ability to function at our best is compromised. Imagine a new marketer pulling consecutive late nights to meet every client request, feeling obligated to accommodate each demand in hopes of securing approval and future work. While the intention behind such efforts might be commendable, the toll on personal well-being often goes unnoticed until exhaustion sets in.

Establishing boundaries in relationships offers a pathway to sustainable happiness. By clearly defining limits, not only do you preserve your own mental and physical health, but you also enhance the quality of interactions with others. Take for example an experienced manager who learns to say no to unnecessary meetings or tasks that could easily be delegated. This act of self-advocacy opens up time for reflection, professional growth, and meaningful engagements. The realization that it's perfectly acceptable to decline requests when they don't align with personal values or capacity leads to more thoughtful contributions that truly matter.

Failing to prioritize personal needs results in a diminished capacity to offer genuine help. Consider the analogy of the airplane safety demonstration, which advises putting on your oxygen mask before assisting others. If you do not first address your own necessities—such as rest, nutrition, and emotional well-being—the quality of support you provide diminishes. A sports coach, eager to guide athletes to success, cannot perform effectively if overwhelmed by fatigue or stress. When basic needs are ignored, frustration, burnout, and inefficiency follow, making it harder to connect with and support those around you authentically.

Moreover, focusing on prioritized and meaningful contributions enables individuals to maintain balance in their lives. Rather than succumbing to the pressures of pleasing everyone, targeting efforts toward areas that align with personal strengths and passions proves far more rewarding. A journalist, for instance, may decide to cover stories about community empowerment rather than being swayed by sensational news topics. This shift empowers the journalist and enriches audiences with content that inspires and informs.

By choosing avenues that foster fulfillment and satisfaction, you unlock the potential to create significant societal impacts. Engaging in activities that uplift the soul feeds positive energy into the broader community. Whether through volunteerism or sharing expertise in seminars or workshops, sparking positive change becomes tangible when actions are rooted in authenticity and purpose. Here, a guideline becomes relevant: Attracting "higher selves" through selfless helping emphasizes not only the importance of benefiting others but also nurtures your spirit in return. Empowering colleagues, mentoring newcomers, or simply listening attentively elevates the workplace environment, fostering respect and collaboration.

Service Through Teaching and Mentorship

One of the most powerful ways to serve others is to teach—especially when what you're teaching is how to see differently.

One of my earliest mentors, Dan Wasserman, did just that. Dan was a brilliant Los Angeles lawyer with a vision decades ahead of his time. He wasn't just an expert in the law—he was a pioneer in global thinking. Long before "globalization" became a buzzword, Dan was flying back and forth between Boston and China, spotting opportunities others couldn't even imagine.

What made Dan such an influential force in my life wasn't just what he achieved—it was how he thought. He taught me to look at my skills, my knowledge, and my deepest desires and ask a powerful question: "Where can I apply this to something that's doing well, something that's stable, or something I believe will thrive in the future?"

Dan lived with a mindset of abundance and service. And like all great teachers, he didn't just tell you how to think—he showed you.

Every time he flew to China, he brought live lobsters from Cape Cod as gifts. They weren't just seafood—they were symbols of connection, generosity, and respect. The gesture was so meaningful, Dan ended up building an entire distribution business just to ship lobsters overseas. A business born out of service. And yes, he made millions.

But he didn't stop there.

On a trip to Israel, Dan noticed chicken feet were being thrown out by the ton—discarded because they couldn't be verified as kosher. But Dan, having spent years in China, knew that chicken feet were a delicacy. What Israel considered waste, China saw as treasure.

So Dan built a bridge.

He got paid to take away the discarded chicken feet in Israel—and paid again to deliver them as a premium product in China. That business? Over $50 million in revenue. But more than the numbers, it was the lesson.

When we stay open to service, we start to see value where others see nothing.

Dan's story is a blueprint for what great mentorship can look like. He didn't just build businesses. He built people. He helped others see what was possible when you aligned your curiosity with your capacity to serve. And that's what teaching really is—it's giving people new lenses.

In every field—sales, marketing, entrepreneurship, sports, media—teaching unlocks exponential impact. When you share what you've learned, you multiply your value. A single lesson can spark a ripple effect across teams, companies, even industries.

Teaching isn't about transferring information. It's about transforming people.

Whether you're mentoring a young entrepreneur or coaching a colleague through a tough patch, every moment of shared knowledge has the potential to change the trajectory of someone's life. And when you empower others to carry that torch forward, the service continues—generation after generation.

Final Insights

Great service doesn't start with other people. It starts with you.

This chapter explored what it means to surround yourself with the right service—service that's meaningful, sustainable, and reciprocal. From the example of a mother who gave with everything she had, to a mentor who built multimillion-dollar companies through observation, generosity, and purpose, we've seen that service isn't about sacrifice alone. It's about strategy.

Guidelines

- Rest isn't laziness—it's preparation. Schedule moments that realign your mindset, body, and spirit.
- Don't give from emptiness. Refill your cup so your contribution flows from joy, not guilt.
- Lead through action—when others see you care for yourself well, they'll learn to do the same.
- Give with purpose, not performance. Ask, "Is this act of service rooted in connection, or in the need for validation?"
- Honor the long game. Sustainable service means protecting your peace while still showing up with generosity and grit.

Takeaways

- Self-care is the foundation of meaningful service—not the opposite of it.
- The best mentors don't just give answers. They help you see value where others see waste.
- Small acts of thoughtful service can become the seed of massive impact.
- You can't lead well or love well if you're running on empty.
- Real service is abundant, not transactional. It grows as it's given.

Ask Yourself

- Am I giving myself the time, space, and care I need to show up as my best self?
- When was the last time I paused to refill my own cup before pouring into others?

- Do I feel energized and fulfilled by the way I'm serving—or am I running on empty?
- Where can I shift from "obligation" to "overflow"?
- What's one small act of meaningful service I can offer today—from a place of wholeness?

The most effective service begins with a well-resourced self. Whether you're in sales, entrepreneurship, media, or leadership, showing up for others at a high level means honoring your own boundaries and energy first. Self-care isn't indulgence—it's infrastructure. It's what lets you stay present, resilient, and impactful in your work, your relationships, and your purpose.

And when service is rooted in overflow rather than depletion, it creates ripples. Small acts—a lobster shared, a lesson taught, a late-night drive with a paper bag dinner—become legacy.

When you align your internal abundance with the right external actions, your life becomes a force for good—not just for those around you, but for generations to come.

PART 2

OWN YOUR TIME, OWN YOUR LIFE

Chapter 5

KNOW WHERE THAT DICK HAS BEEN

Relativity of the Past

Understanding where that proverbial "dick" has been means taking a hard look at the people and behaviors—both around us and within us—that have negatively influenced our journey. Sometimes, the "dick" is someone else: a toxic boss, a manipulative friend, a harsh critic from your past. But just as often, the "dick" is you. It's your ego, your fear, your insecurity, or the way you've treated yourself or others when operating from a place of lack. Either way, these influences leave a mark. They shape how we think, how we feel, and how we show up in business and life.

These unexamined patterns can resurface when we least expect them—sabotaging relationships, derailing performance, or clouding judgment. That's why it's not just helpful, but essential, to pause and reflect: Where have we been? Who has shaped us—for better or worse? And how do we begin to separate ourselves from the patterns, people, and mindsets that no longer serve us?

If we want to grow, we have to stop doing business with the "dicks" out there. And just as importantly, we have to stop doing business with the one inside.

I'll never forget the time I invited Dr. Sangeeta Sahi, one of my earliest mentors and the person who introduced me to meditation and quantum healing, to lead a workshop with my team. We were diving deep into the unseen—the energy we carry, the quantum inheritance passed down through generations, not just genetically, but energetically.

At one point during the session, Dr. Sangeeta paused, looked at me, and said something that completely caught me off guard.

"Oh my goodness," she said, almost in disbelief. "You carry an energy that says you're stupid."

I laughed. "C'mon, Sangeeta," I said. "I can understand carrying insecurities. I mean, if someone made fun of my nose when I was a kid, sure, I might have been self-conscious. But today? I just tell people I don't have a big nose. I have a small face."

But she wasn't laughing.

"No, no," she said. "It's not that you think you're stupid. It's that you carry an energy that you're stupid."

That's when we started peeling back the layers of my past. And it hit me. Hard.

I was a hyperactive kid. I had five siblings, and my single mom worked relentlessly to keep things together. My grandmother, who helped raise us, was a disciplinarian—old-school, tough love. And like most kids bouncing off the walls at age five or six, I'd often come to her and say, "Grandma, I'm bored."

She had one reply, always the same: "Only stupid people get bored. Smart people think of things to do."

Now, to a kid, that might sound harmless—maybe even motivational. But when someone you admire says it over and over, it doesn't just land in your mind. It seeps into your energy.

Without realizing it, I spent years surrounding myself with people who made me feel smart. That was my comfort zone. That was my validation. I chose rooms where I could be the smartest person—not because I was arrogant, but because I was afraid of what it felt like not to be.

It wasn't until much later, in work like this with Dr. Sangeeta, that I understood what was really happening. The energy we carry often runs deeper than what we think or even consciously believe. It's the frequency underneath—the signal beneath the story—that creates interference. That energy becomes our magnet. It draws in the people, situations, and rooms we walk into.

Today, I live by a different rule: If I'm not the dumbest person in the room, I'm in the wrong room. Growth requires humility. Progress demands presence. And the energy we bring into each moment will always determine who we become.

So be careful what you say, what you believe, and—most importantly—what you feel. Because what you feel is what you become.

This chapter explores how the past continues to shape us—not as an anchor, but as a launchpad. It's a deep dive into the relativity of time and influence, showing how the "dicks" we've met, or been, leave patterns that only awareness can unravel. Through stories of entrepreneurship, media, and leadership, we'll reframe missteps as momentum, and see how releasing regret opens the door to reinvention.

The Relativity of Time and Our Perception

One of the most powerful lessons I've learned in life—and continue to learn—is about relativity. Not in the Einstein sense, but in the emotional, human sense. Relativity is the meaning we assign to our experiences. And when it comes to our past, that meaning can either empower us or imprison us.

So many people are held back not by what happened to them, but by what they believe it meant. We build narratives about the past—stories that shape our self-image—and then live inside those stories, often unaware of how much they influence our present.

But here's the truth: You will never outachieve your self-image. You will never outperform your own imagination of who you are.

One of the most unexpected teachers of this truth was the legendary pitcher Vida Blue.

We'd brought Vida in for an appearance. The room was electric—lines of people waiting to shake his hand, snap a photo, share a memory. One after another, they told him, "You're the legend. You're the GOAT. The greatest pitcher of all time."

I stood back and watched it all unfold. Then Vida looked at me, smiled, and said something I'll never forget.

"The older I get, the better I was."

At first, I laughed. But the more I thought about it, the more I understood what he was really saying. He wasn't just being cheeky—he was assigning new meaning to the past. Not to rewrite history, but to enjoy it. To reframe it with reverence and humor. To let it lift his future, not limit it.

We all have that same power. We give meaning to everything—especially our past. So if you're going to assign meaning, make sure it serves you. Don't let an old story shrink your self-image. Rewrite it. Own it. Let it expand your sense of what's possible.

Vida's story is more than just a moment of charm. It's a reminder that our past isn't fixed. Its influence is relative—relative to the meaning we give it.

Whether you're building a business, running a sales team, launching a creative campaign, or leading a locker room, the pressure to constantly perform can make past failures feel like weights around your ankles. But when you reframe those failures as teachers, they become fuel. A lost client becomes the moment your communication sharpened. A public flop becomes the foundation of your next bold idea.

This isn't just positive spin. It's practice. Reframing the past as purposeful takes intentionality. But it's one of the most powerful ways to rewire your energy and reclaim your momentum.

Popular culture captures this truth in unexpected places. In *Kung Fu Panda*, Po's journey toward self-belief doesn't hinge on changing the past—it hinges on changing what the past means to him. He learns to embrace his oddball history, his quirks, and his setbacks, turning them into strengths. The moral? The past only limits you if you let it. When you embrace it, it becomes your superpower.

For professionals in any space where innovation and visibility matter, this idea is vital. It's easy to obsess over what went wrong. But if you adopt a Po-like lens, you'll find opportunity where others see failure. You'll turn pressure into creativity. You'll let your history be a springboard instead of a ceiling.

But reframing of this nature isn't automatic. It takes work. It means challenging old scripts and being intentional about the energy you bring forward. One simple but powerful practice? Revisit your past decisions through the lens of learning and leverage. Ask: What did that experience teach me? How did it shape who I am? What part of that story do I want to carry forward—and what part am I ready to release?

Remember: The older you get, the better your story can become. Not because the facts change—but because you do.

Changing the Past Through Perspective

Reflecting on our past can feel like looking into a mirror; sometimes the image seems distorted, showing us the mistakes and missteps that we wish to forget. However, if we can alter our perspective, those same reflections can become valuable guides for personal growth and success. Embracing past mistakes as lessons rather than failures empowers us in profound ways.

Consider how often we chastise ourselves for errors—whether it's missing a crucial deadline or mishandling an important meeting. It's essential to recognize that these mistakes are not just blunders but opportunities to learn. The key is to dissect what went wrong and understand how to avoid similar pitfalls in the future. Imagine you're an athlete who has just lost an important game; analyzing your performance allows you to identify weaknesses and improve. This process transforms regret into momentum, propelling you forward.

Take successful athletes, for instance. Many have faced heart-breaking losses early in their careers. Yet, instead of dwelling on failure, they focus ahead. Michael Jordan, widely regarded as one of the greatest basketball players of all time, was cut from his high school team. Rather than allowing this to define him, he used it as motivation to hone his skills and eventually ascend to greatness.

This mindset shift illustrates the power of focusing forward while acknowledging past setbacks as stepping stones.

These experiences teach us that altering our view of the past reshapes its impact on our lives. When we see challenges as stepping stones rather than stumbling blocks, we pave the way for resilience and creativity. Learning from past experiences helps prevent repeated mistakes. Each experience offers lessons, serving as road maps to navigate future obstacles. By consciously evaluating our actions, we become more adept at making informed decisions. Reflecting on past campaigns or projects can lead to innovative solutions and drive future success.

Furthermore, mounting regrets can be overwhelming, hindering our ability to make sound decisions. The weight of what-ifs and could-have-beens can anchor us in self-doubt. By shifting our perspective, we alleviate these burdens, allowing space for clarity and progress. For instance, a marketing manager who regrets a failed campaign might feel paralyzed by the fear of repeating the mistake. However, viewing the failure as a learning opportunity opens doors to creative strategies that may ultimately achieve greater success.

A critical approach to managing regrets involves reframing them. Instead of seeing them as negative marks on our life's timeline, we should view them as chapters filled with rich insights. Changing our perspective does not erase what happened but rather alters its significance, reducing its grip over our present actions. This mental shift is vital for decision-making, enabling professionals to respond proactively rather than reactively.

In the competitive worlds of sales, marketing, advertising, and beyond, the pressure to succeed is relentless. Mistakes are inevitable, yet they are also invaluable. Imagine a salesperson losing a major deal due to a strategic misstep. While initially disheartening, the experience provides insights about client preferences and market demands, enriching future interactions. Such instances highlight the transformative potential of embracing errors as educational tools.

It's crucial for individuals in management roles to foster an environment where past mistakes are openly discussed and leveraged for collective growth. This creates a culture where employees are encouraged to experiment and innovate without the paralyzing fear of failure. It's akin to how sports teams review game footage to refine strategies and bolster confidence. After all, a team that learns from its losses is often the one best poised for victory when it matters most.

This transformative approach requires letting go of perfectionism. Perfection is a myth that stifles creativity and innovation. Accepting that mistakes are part of the journey instills a growth mindset, enabling both individuals and organizations to evolve continuously. In entrepreneurship, failure is almost a rite of passage, a test of resilience and adaptability. The stories of entrepreneurs who failed multiple times before achieving success exemplify the power of perseverance and learning.

Letting go of regrets necessitates adopting a mindset that values progress over perfection. Professionals who understand this appreciate the nuances of their journeys, recognizing that every setback offers new knowledge. They are not deterred by past missteps, nor do they dwell excessively on them; instead, they use those experiences as fuel to forge ahead.

To manage the impact of past events effectively, consider focusing on three main guidelines: First, accept responsibility for your actions without succumbing to guilt or blame. This empowers you to move forward constructively. Second, engage in honest reflection to extract valuable lessons from each experience. Finally, actively apply these insights to future endeavors, ensuring that your past informs—rather than obstructs—your path to success.

Empowerment Through Accountability and Truth

As we've talked about, understanding how our past shapes our present and future is crucial. The key to transforming negative narratives from our past into positive forces in our lives lies in honesty.

Being truthful with yourself is the first step in mitigating the impact of negative past experiences. Each of us has moments we're not proud of or situations we wish had gone differently. However, recognizing these moments with honesty allows us to distance ourselves from their negative influences. By confronting the truth, we can prevent past mistakes from continuing to shape our current decisions and attitudes. It is similar to clearing up a cloudy lens to view life more clearly, making informed and objective choices.

Reframing experiences as beneficial challenges rather than getting caught in their negativity is important. Instead of viewing a lost promotion or a failed campaign as a setback, consider them as stepping stones that offer valuable insights. These experiences provide lessons that refine your skills and pave the way for future success. Viewing them as challenges encourages you to tackle them head-on, armed with newfound knowledge and determination. This proactive approach fosters resilience and adaptability—traits highly valued in any professional environment.

Honesty also plays a vital role in preventing negative perceptions from persisting. When left unexamined, these perceptions can distort reality, making it difficult to break free from a cycle of negativity. By honestly acknowledging our feelings and thoughts about past events, we gain power over them. Rather than allowing them to dictate our actions or mindset, we consciously reshape them into more constructive narratives. This transformation is not instantaneous but becomes more profound over time with consistent practice.

Moreover, honest reflection enables us to redefine negative past events as positive learning experiences. As we delve into past incidents with an open mind, we often find valuable lessons hidden beneath the surface. Perhaps a challenging project taught you the importance of collaboration, or a client dispute helped you develop better communication skills. Recognizing these insights promotes growth and empowers you to approach similar situations more effectively in the future. This reframing process helps shift focus from what went wrong to what was gained, fostering a feeling of gratitude even for difficult experiences.

Incorporating honesty into our introspection doesn't mean dwelling on past mistakes. Instead, it's about accepting responsibility and striving for continuous improvement. In the world of sports and entertainment, athletes and performers are familiar with reviewing their performances to identify areas for enhancement. Similarly, professionals in any field can benefit from periodically assessing their journey, using past experiences as benchmarks for personal and professional growth. This ongoing process encourages a mindset centered around progress rather than perfection.

The importance of surrounding yourself with positive influences cannot be underestimated when transforming past narratives. A supportive network of friends, colleagues, and mentors acts as a sounding board for your thoughts, offering encouragement and diverse perspectives. Engaging with others who share similar values can reinforce honest reflections and provide motivation to strive for excellence. Creating this network offers guidance and accountability, further ensuring that past experiences are harnessed productively rather than weighing you down.

Here's a simple guideline: Regularly reflect on significant experiences and their impacts on your life. Analyze both positive and negative events, noting the emotions and lessons they evoke. Consider whether you've acknowledged the true nature of these occurrences and how they influence your beliefs and decisions today. Practice candid self-assessment without judgment, permitting yourself to learn and grow continuously. Engage with positive influences in your life who encourage open dialogue and offer alternative viewpoints. Use these conversations as opportunities to explore different interpretations of past events, broadening your understanding and enhancing your personal development.

Utilizing Sports and Stories as Perspectives

Sports narratives often serve as powerful illustrations of overcoming past setbacks, demonstrating how individuals and teams can transform defeats into victories. Throughout history, sports have provided us with countless examples where athletes have bounced back from losses, using their previous experiences as stepping stones rather than stumbling blocks. This transformation is not just about the physical game but a mental shift that changes their trajectory.

Consider the iconic comeback stories in sports—narratives that have inspired many beyond the field of play. From Michael Jordan's return to the NBA after a brief retirement to Serena Williams defying odds by reaching the Grand Slam finals post-injury and childbirth, these stories are emblematic of resilience. Such tales remind us that setbacks, while initially disheartening, are not the final say. Instead, they become the starting point for a greater journey.

Moreover, the personal journeys of these athletes highlight a deep collective belief in surpassing past limits, which often extends to entire teams. This collective spirit is evident in team sports, where the shared past of failures can galvanize a group toward success. The Boston Red Sox, for instance, finally broke the "Curse of the Bambino" by winning the World Series in 2004 after an 86-year drought, rewriting their narrative through teamwork and perseverance. Their triumph was a product of not just athletic skill but an unwavering belief in moving beyond historical limitations.

The power of belief in reshaping outcomes can't be understated. Teams often thrive on this sense of unity and shared purpose, which strengthens their resolve to achieve what seemed impossible. This tenet of belief and determination is essential in any fast-paced profession, where challenges are inevitable, and bouncing back from setbacks determines long-term success.

Sports also offer numerous personal anecdotes demonstrating these principles. Take Malcolm Butler's story, for example. In the NFL Super Bowl XLIX, Butler made a pivotal interception that clinched victory for the New England Patriots. Yet, his path to this moment was far from smooth.

Undrafted and initially not in the spotlight, Butler trained relentlessly, seizing opportunities and learning from every potential misstep. His miraculous interception stands as testament to how perseverance and preparation can shift outcomes dramatically.

This is a vivid reminder that what appears to be chance is often the result of years of dedication and the ability to learn from past struggles. In competitive environments, whether on the field or in the boardroom, it is crucial to internalize the notion that setbacks are lessons cloaked in hardship. They impart critical insights that, when leveraged correctly, can catalyze extraordinary achievements.

Guidelines can help channel these insights effectively. Understanding the importance of shifting energy from lament to action, embracing setbacks as learning opportunities, and fostering conscious beliefs aimed at future successes can pivot past failures into foundational strengths. These practices are not confined to sports; they resonate in any scenario where professionals strive to overturn negative past judgments and propel themselves toward future potential.

Letting Go of Blame, Shame, and Justification

In our professional journeys, we inevitably encounter situations and people that can leave us burdened with blame or shame. Holding on to these negative emotions is like being stuck in a time warp, constantly reliving moments that prevent us from moving forward. Whether it's a failed deal, a misstep in strategy, or a moment of conflict with a colleague, dwelling on the past can be a powerful anchor, rooting us to a spot we're eager to escape.

Consider how an athlete might feel after missing a crucial shot that costs their team the game. If they continue to replay that moment in their minds, focusing only on the failure, it becomes a shackle, hindering their future performance. This isn't just about sports; it's about any professional field where mistakes are part of the growth process. The key is to understand when these reflections cease to be constructive and instead become detrimental.

The path to freeing ourselves from this emotional baggage begins with a conscious act of letting go. This doesn't mean forgetting or pretending events never happened. Instead, it involves acknowledging these moments as part of our journey and then choosing not to let them define us. Releasing these emotions facilitates a sense of freedom, allowing us to navigate toward positive change. Imagine how liberating it is for a marketing executive who learns from a failed campaign rather than internalizing it as a personal flaw. They turn the experience into a stepping stone toward innovation and creativity.

This newfound freedom opens up space for expecting good outcomes. Shifting focus from past negativity to future potential transforms our approach to challenges. By anticipating positive results, we start to see opportunities where there once were obstacles. Take, for example, a salesperson who lost a significant client. If they dwell on this loss, it could impede their confidence. But by choosing to expect positive engagement in future pitches, they are more likely to find success and attract new clients. This mindset shift is crucial in high-pressure environments where resilience is often the best tool at our disposal.

Crafting empowering past narratives can significantly impact our future fulfillment. When we reframe our past experiences in a way that highlights lessons learned and strengths developed, we empower ourselves to take control of our narratives. For instance, consider a journalist who faces criticism for their coverage. Instead of focusing on the critique and letting it stunt their career, they assess the feedback constructively, leading to improved reporting skills and a stronger professional reputation. This approach allows us to view our past as a series of growth opportunities rather than failures to be feared.

While reflecting on past interactions, particularly those involving difficult personalities or conflicts, it is essential to defy collective beliefs that may have shaped our interpretations. Many professionals remain trapped by societal expectations or judgments about how certain situations should unfold. By questioning and redefining these norms, we gain the ability to create a more personal and authentic narrative that aligns with our values and aspirations.

Moreover, taking accountability for personal freedom plays a critical role in the process of releasing negative emotions tied to the past. Acknowledging our mistakes without self-condemnation empowers us to make conscious choices about how we wish to proceed. It requires courage to accept that, while we cannot change past actions, we can shape our responses moving forward. When entrepreneurs face setbacks, it is often their acceptance of responsibility that fuels their drive to innovate and succeed despite previous challenges.

Ultimately, understanding the relativity of our past and its impact on our present and future is an ongoing journey. It involves continuous learning and adapting, with the goal of crafting a narrative that serves us rather than hinders us. Letting go of blame and shame, expecting positive outcomes, and owning our past empower us to move confidently into the future, armed with the wisdom we've gained along the way. This transformation is available to everyone, regardless of profession or position, enabling a life that is both fulfilling and fearless.

Final Insights

It's funny how the relativity of the past can shape so much of our identity—especially the perceptions, conditions, and judgments that others place on us when we're too young to question them.

Growing up, I was surrounded by a family that lived and breathed academics. The joke in my house was that the fetus wasn't considered fully developed until after graduate school. A "B" on a report card wasn't a grade—it was a crisis. Expectations were sky-high, and comparisons were constant. Not just in my immediate family, but across cousins, aunts, uncles—everyone.

The pressure was relentless. So much so that a few of my cousins, even some who graduated from Harvard summa cum laude, later took their own lives. That's how heavy the burden of conditional love and performance-based identity had become. The message was clear: Your worth is tied to how well you perform. Anything less than perfect isn't good enough.

That story could have written my future. But I decided to rewrite it.

Even now, if I went to a family reunion and told them I'd gone to the Ivy League and graduated at the top of my class, I might get a polite nod. But if I said I was the only one in our extended family to ever play a college sport? That I played football? That might actually get some real attention. Not because it fit the traditional mold of success—but because it was mine.

Over time, something shifted. Those same relatives started expressing appreciation—not because I met their standards, but because I had the courage to follow my own. Because I defined success for myself. Because I chose authenticity over applause.

This is the power of reframing. The past is relative—but it's also powerful. And the meaning we attach to it either holds us back or sets us free.

When we rewrite our past with purpose, we reclaim our future with possibility.

Guidelines

- See each mistake as a stepping stone, not a stop sign. Like Jordan missing game-winners before he made them, failure often precedes greatness.
- Carrying regret keeps you anchored. Let go of guilt and make space for creativity and courage.
- Learn the lesson, then move forward. Reflection brings growth; rumination brings stagnation.

Takeaways

- The past is not fixed—it's flexible.
- You will never outperform your self-image.
- Growth begins when you replace blame with ownership.
- A story rewritten is a future reclaimed.
- There is no "right" version of success—only the one that's true for you.

Ask Yourself

- Do I view my past mistakes as proof of failure or fuel for growth?
- What's one challenge I've faced that shaped who I am today?
- Am I still holding on to blame—or have I replaced it with accountability and optimism?

When you shift the meaning of the past, you shift the direction of your life. What once limited you can now lift you. And in that shift, there's freedom. There's progress. There's power.

That's what I learned with Dr. Sangeeta. It wasn't just about what I thought—I wasn't carrying a thought that I was stupid. I was carrying the *energy* of it. Because I had absorbed a story long ago and never questioned it. But the moment I did, the moment I rewrote it, everything changed. I stopped letting that energy choose my rooms, shape my self-image, and limit my potential.

You can do the same.

Because your past isn't the problem. The meaning you've given it is.

And the beautiful thing is—*you* get to choose a new meaning. One that frees you. One that fits you. One that fuels who you're becoming.

Chapter 6

ARE YOU A DICK?

Relativity of the Present

The moment I realized I had gone bankrupt didn't come with a phone call or a letter. It came when I looked around and saw that my basement had a basement. That's how far I had fallen. I couldn't even get out of bed. Not because I was physically unable—but because I had to do something that felt impossible: go tell my mom that, not only had I lost more than a hundred million dollars, but I had lost her house too. She was going to have to move because of my mistakes.

I lay there, tears soaking the pillow, crushed under the weight of shame, fear, and self-blame. I remember repeating the same questions in my head: *How could I have let this happen? Why me? Why am I being punished?*

And most painfully: *How am I ever going to come back from this?*

As I stared blankly at the ceiling, I turned on the TV just to feel something other than failure. What I got wasn't distraction. It was divine direction. *Rocky* was on. The original. It was the final round.

Rocky, bloodied and broken, lay flat on the mat. Apollo had just knocked him down again. Everyone—his trainer, Paulie—was yelling, "Stay down, Rocky! Stay down!" Adrian was crying. The crowd was shouting, "Get up, Rocky! Get up!"

And then Rocky looked up.

In that moment, I stopped crying.

Not because the pain had passed. But because the message was clear: Get up. Be here. Right now.

Navigating the complexities of balancing present living with future fear is a challenge many professionals face—especially in high-pressure worlds like sales, entrepreneurship, entertainment, and leadership. It's easy to get stuck in the past or panic about the future. But the only moment we can actually act in is now.

This chapter explores what it means to live in the present with full awareness—and what happens when we don't. Because here's the truth: You can't lead from your past and you can't perform from your future. You can only create, connect, decide, and rise from where your feet are.

The Rocky moment taught me this. I didn't need to win the match that day. I just needed to get up. I needed to stop reliving what had gone wrong and stop catastrophizing what might happen next. I needed to choose the present. Not just endure it—inhabit it.

We'll dive into why that kind of presence is more than a mindset. It's a muscle. And in this chapter, we'll show how learning to train it—through simple choices, daily habits, and moment-to-moment awareness—can transform how you work, how you lead, and how you live. Whether you're navigating a comeback, chasing a dream, or just trying to stay sane in a high-stakes environment, the question is this: Are you being the best version of yourself, now, in the present?

The Futility of Worrying About the Future

It's all too easy to fall into the trap of worrying excessively about the future. We've all done it. We've all been there. And we'll all be there again. But foreboding is a terrible investment strategy. It burns time, drains energy, and delivers nothing in return.

Imagine spending hours stressed about a scenario that may never come to pass—it's like putting your money into a slot machine that's never paid out. That mental energy could be used for something else—something that actually moves you forward today.

Now, look—I get it. Most professionals, especially in high-stakes industries like sales, marketing, and entrepreneurship, survive on foresight. Strategy is oxygen. Planning ahead is part of what makes us effective. But when that planning turns into obsession—when every quiet moment becomes a mental spiral about what *might* go wrong two quarters from now—it's no longer preparation. It's paralysis.

Let me give you a real example. I once worked with a startup founder—we'll call him Leo—who had just closed his Series A. Big milestone. But instead of celebrating the win or focusing on the product rollout, he was already spiraling about Series B. He was losing sleep over whether the next funding round would come fast enough, whether competitors were secretly hiring better engineers, whether AI would kill their road map entirely.

I remember sitting across from him and saying, "Leo, you haven't even launched your core product yet—and you're already trying to solve for problems two years down the line. What if you just showed up for your users today?"

He looked at me and said something I'll never forget: "But if I stop worrying, won't I fall behind?"

That mindset is the trap.

He wasn't falling behind because he *wasn't* worrying.

He was falling behind because he was worrying *instead* of building.

When we live too far in the future, we lose sight of what's real right now. The conversation with a customer. The insight from your team. The spark of a new idea. Those are the things that actually shape the future—not the late-night hypotheticals keeping you up.

So here's the shift: Planning is useful. Worry is not. Strategy builds. Anxiety stalls.

And the more you obsess about the horizon, the more likely you are to trip over your own feet.

It's vital to understand that trusting future solutions doesn't equate to neglecting present responsibilities. Many times, we hear advice like "everything will work out," but it's essential to differentiate between genuine faith in future solutions and sheer complacency. Believing future solutions will arise should inspire problem-solving initiatives now rather than justify inaction. Trust can serve as a motivational tool when burdened with current challenges. It should empower individuals to make decisive moves with their available resources.

This trust, cleverly utilized, helps maintain focus and drive without being paralyzed by hypothetical problems. Take a marketing manager dealing with brand image issues post-controversy. If he puts all efforts into correcting the narrative today while confidently believing in the power of tomorrow's outreach campaigns, he's channeling trust effectively. His belief fuels today's actions, reinforcing his commitment to existing challenges while keeping sight of future recovery possibilities.

Moreover, living responsibly in the present profoundly impacts the future. It's not merely about having an optimistic outlook; it's about actively shaping your trajectory through decisions made today.

Professionals need to internalize the principle: Aligning present choices with desired future outcomes ensures a sound strategy for long-term success. For example, consider a seasoned journalist who focuses on building strong networks within the industry. Her connections, established through interactive engagements and diligent reporting today, pave the way for career advancement tomorrow.

This principle applies to everyone regardless of their profession. Athletes train consistently to enhance their skills today; actors rehearse tirelessly despite potential casting risks; sales executives nurture client relationships knowing these seeds will bloom into successful partnerships. Such dedication shapes a brighter future from the substance and quality of daily actions.

Guidelines that facilitate living fully in the present are particularly relevant here. Firstly, develop clear objectives rooted in present realities. Defining short-term goals provides clarity and encourages proactive steps toward achievement. Secondly, exercise mindfulness—a practice that keeps awareness centered on the current moment and promotes better emotional regulation. By acknowledging present circumstances, one can take informed actions without becoming overwhelmed by external uncertainties.

Additionally, embrace positive thinking patterns. While difficult situations may prevail, maintaining a constructive attitude equips one with resilience, enabling adaptive responses to immediate concerns. Surrounding yourself with supportive influences, such as mentors or colleagues who inspire and motivate, fosters an environment conducive to personal growth and career development. Relationships built on mutual encouragement fortify one against external pressures, reinforcing the importance of focusing on strengths and opportunities existent now.

Finally, embody flexibility in both thought and action.

Recognizing that change is intrinsic to life allows individuals to adapt strategies based on evolving scenarios, preventing rigid adherence to plans that no longer serve their purpose. Receptiveness to new ideas and willingness to experiment instills confidence and optimism, elements fundamental to managing present tasks effectively and ensuring future readiness.

Liberation Through Present Awareness

Embracing the present moment is a powerful act of generosity, one that surpasses all gestures motivated by past obligations or future expectations. To truly give in the present means to invest yourself entirely—your attention, your energy, and your presence—in what's happening right now. This kind of involvement stems from acknowledging that our greatest contributions are often made when we anchor ourselves in the moment. When you're in a meeting, for example, being genuinely engaged can lead to more innovative ideas and stronger connections with colleagues. In contrast, if your mind is preoccupied with past mistakes or future worries, those opportunities may slip by unnoticed.

Understanding that time is an illusion can be liberating. We often think of time as a linear progression, yet the only true reality we have is this moment. The notions of yesterday and tomorrow are constructs of the human mind; what we really possess is "now." Think about athletes performing at their best. They don't succeed because they dwell on past failures or future challenges, but because they're present, focused solely on executing their current play. This focus enables them to respond to the unpredictability of their environment effectively, showcasing how deeply living in the now can enhance performance.

The idea that we can learn from the past but cannot change it offers a sense of freedom. Many people spend considerable mental energy revisiting past events, wishing they had acted differently. However, what the past truly offers is a chance for learning, not reliving. By understanding and accepting this, you liberate yourself to focus on making immediate, impactful decisions. In professional settings, this shift in mindset can transform how you approach your work. Instead of being bogged down by how a previous sales pitch went wrong, use that experience to refine your strategy in real-time interactions, thus improving outcomes in the here and now.

Relinquishing the grip of past regrets frees us to fully engage with what's right in front of us. When we're anchored to what was, we risk drifting past what could be.

I once knew a former athlete who couldn't stop reliving the glory days—high school championships, trophies, records, the whole thing. Every conversation eventually turned into a highlight reel. But while he was stuck replaying the past, life was moving forward without him. Opportunities came and went. New roles appeared, but he couldn't see them—because his identity was still wearing yesterday's jersey.

It wasn't until he finally let go of who he had been that he discovered who he could become. A coach. A mentor. A leader. And in stepping into those roles, he found something bigger than a trophy—he found purpose. He started shaping futures instead of replaying his past.

Letting go doesn't mean forgetting.

It means making space for what's next.

Additionally, there's a practical dimension to embracing the present—it allows for clearer goal manifestation. Being present doesn't mean ignoring your dreams and ambitions. Quite the contrary, living in the now actually facilitates the realization of long-term goals.

By taking consistent actions aligned with your larger objectives, while grounded in the present, you remain flexible enough to adapt as circumstances evolve. For instance, marketers aiming to launch a successful campaign must tread the fine line between planning for future milestones and responding to real-time feedback. This balance ensures that their strategies remain dynamic and effective.

Furthermore, embracing present experiences cultivates a deeper appreciation for life's nuances. It encourages us to savor each moment and find joy in simple pleasures, a mindset that fosters resilience against stress and adversity. Imagine a performer onstage, completely absorbed in their song, connecting with the audience in a way that transcends words. This synergy, born from being fully present, not only captivates the audience but also enriches the performer's experience, contributing to a fulfilling career.

However, living in the present isn't about ignoring potential risks or challenges. It's about confronting them with a clear mind and a considered approach. Sales professionals, for example, face constant pressure to meet targets and adapt to market shifts. Those who master the art of focusing on current priorities while maintaining an awareness of future trends are better equipped to make strategic decisions that benefit both their clients and their careers in the long run.

To harness the ability to manifest desires through present action, it's critical to understand the value of incremental progress. Small, deliberate steps taken today lay the foundation for larger successes tomorrow. Entrepreneurs, particularly, thrive in environments where quick thinking and decisive action define success. By establishing a series of achievable interim goals, they navigate complex landscapes with agility and foresight, ensuring sustainable growth while remaining anchored in the present.

Finally, financial and emotional goals also hinge on current actions. Making prudent financial choices requires mindfulness about spending and investment habits in the present. Emotional well-being, too, flourishes when nurtured with present-moment awareness. Balancing immediate responsibilities with future aspirations creates harmony between personal satisfaction and professional achievement.

The Present Focus Versus Past Glories and Future Concerns

What I've come to realize is that it's not our past failures, setbacks, or even our biggest mistakes that keep us from reaching our potential. It's our commitment—or lack of it—that determines how far we'll go. So often, it's the *relativity of the present*, the way we show up in the moment, that defines the energy we give to our future. And that's what separates those who rise from those who retreat.

I'll never forget a moment that brought this lesson home. My daughter's friend Sophie didn't make the cheerleading squad her freshman year. She was devastated. Most people would've thrown in the towel right there. She was laughed at, whispered about, made to feel like she didn't belong.

But Sophie didn't fold.

She doubled down. She started taking private lessons. Every day after school and every weekend, she was practicing. Her commitment was unwavering. By her sophomore year, she nearly landed a varsity spot. By the end of that season, she wasn't just on the team—she was the varsity captain.

The same people who once scoffed at her were now applauding her.

That's what commitment looks like. Not perfection. Not instant success. Just the daily decision to keep going, no matter what anyone else says.

Now compare that with a former baseball player I knew. He had real talent—enough to be drafted. But instead of putting in the work during his rookie season, he was already fantasizing about endorsements, brand deals, and what kind of car he'd buy once he made it big. His mind was five years ahead, but his game was two steps behind. While others were grinding through reps and film, he was scrolling dream homes and scouting luxury watches. And the more he looked forward, the less he showed up in the now.

He didn't last the season.

The difference between Sophie and the ballplayer wasn't ability. It was focus. She was grounded in the present, making daily deposits of discipline. He was living in a highlight reel that hadn't been earned yet. One was building a future. The other was borrowing from it. We all do this. We romanticize the past. We obsess about the future. But the people who grow—who succeed—are the ones who learn to be fully present. They show up today. They do the work today. They stay committed, even when no one's watching.

Because the present is where your future is born.

Many professionals inadvertently fall into the trap of defining themselves by their previous milestones. These accomplishments, while noteworthy, might create a false sense of security or even entitlement. Imagine an athlete who once broke records but now rests on prior laurels. By constantly dwelling on those past victories, they might neglect current training and development opportunities, ultimately stunting their career progression. Success should serve as a stepping stone, not a resting place. This mindset allows for continuous growth and adaptation to new challenges.

Shifting our focus to handling obstacles, it's essential to

recognize how perceiving challenges as unmanageable can lead to failure, particularly off the court. In sports, players are trained to evaluate and overcome hurdles systematically. Yet, in professional settings, these skills don't always translate seamlessly. A marketer facing declining campaign performance might feel overwhelmed, interpreting this as an insurmountable issue rather than a problem to dissect and address. When obstacles appear daunting, it's easy to spiral into anxiety and stagnation, further exacerbating the situation. Here's where practice in skill-building becomes invaluable. Regularly honing your skills, whether through courses, workshops, or real-life problem-solving, ensures resilience and enhances capability to tackle whatever comes next.

Furthermore, athletes' success often hinges on their ability to stay accountable and motivated in the present moment. Consider an inspiring story: Sara, a young tennis player whose initial tournaments were riddled with losses. Instead of clinging to defeat and letting self-doubt take hold, she decided to view each match as a learning opportunity. Sara documented her strengths and weaknesses after every game, setting small, achievable goals to improve her performance. This approach required consistent effort and attention to her current needs and strategies, rather than past failures or distant triumphs. Her steadfast dedication paid off, transforming her into a formidable competitor.

This narrative underpins the importance of accountability. In any profession, holding oneself responsible for daily tasks and objectives prevents apathy and fosters progress. Accountability isn't merely about tracking metrics or hitting targets; it's about embracing a mindset that encourages action, reflection, and adjustment. Professionals who embody this approach tend to have greater job satisfaction and achieve higher levels of success by prioritizing what's actionable today over what was or could be.

Practicing and improving skills for success demands a structured approach. Start by setting specific, realistic goals that you can incorporate into your routine. Identify key areas where improvement is needed and seek out resources—be it seminars, online courses, or mentorship—that cater to these needs. Keep track of your progress regularly and celebrate small victories to build momentum. Importantly, remain flexible and open to change, as the path to success is rarely linear.

While conquering obstacles and sharpening skills are vital, maintaining motivation often circles back to mindfulness—being fully engaged in the here and now. For individuals working in high-stress environments, like advertising executives managing multiple campaigns, the pressure to perform can be overwhelming. Cultivating techniques such as meditation or mindful breaks during the workday helps to center thoughts on the present. These practices can reduce stress and increase mental clarity, enhancing both productivity and creativity.

Ultimately, thriving in the present doesn't mean ignoring past successes or future plans; rather, it encompasses leveraging them to inform current decisions and actions. By building on past lessons without becoming complacent and preparing for potential futures without succumbing to fear, professionals across industries can navigate their careers with confidence and grace. Embracing the present moment serves as an essential strategy for overcoming life's myriad hurdles and paving the way for long-term success.

Adopting the Power of Now

Is your workplace competitive? I'm guessing there's a good chance that it is. And those competitive environments can easily lead to imagined problems that drain our happiness, overshadowing the present moment's experiences. We've all been there—caught in thoughts of what might happen if a deal fails or a campaign flops. However, these worst-fear scenarios rarely manifest, illustrating how they only distract us from enjoying life as it is happening.

Consider a salesperson who spends hours worrying about losing a client meeting. This foreboding thought might influence her mood, making her interactions with colleagues less pleasant. Instead of focusing on preparing constructively for the meeting, she finds herself ruminating over worst-case scenarios. If she directed this energy toward embracing the preparation process, the actual experience could become more enjoyable and productive. Imagined problems are like shadows—they seem ominous until true light shines upon them, dissipating their presence.

While the professional world demands perfection, clinging too tightly to that ideal can be counterproductive. We must recognize that imperfections are part of the human tapestry, offering opportunities for growth and learning. Embracing these flaws and the authenticity of present experiences leads us to greater satisfaction. For instance, an entrepreneur launching a new product may worry incessantly about every minor defect. Yet, by accepting that early versions have room for improvement, they can focus on user feedback, fostering a better connection with customers and refining the product.

Take the sporting industry as a further example. Athletes frequently face failures and setbacks. Those who excel learn to embrace these moments, understanding that each stumble is a stride toward mastery. They don't conceal their weaknesses but use them as stepping stones for future triumphs. By doing so, they maintain a balance between ambition and acceptance, which is equally applicable in the office setting. A manager acknowledging missteps openly creates an environment where team members feel safe to do the same, promoting innovative problem-solving and collaboration.

Moreover, surrounding ourselves with positive influences significantly enhances our experience of the present. Imagine working in an advertising agency where cynicism runs rampant; creativity stagnates under persistent negativity. Conversely, an environment buzzing with encouragement and constructive feedback fosters innovation and personal contentment. Positivity breeds positivity, creating a fulfilling work culture. Encouraging uplifting relationships both personally and professionally ensures that the present moment remains enriching and productive.

For those in media and journalism, maintaining a balance with positive influences is crucial amid the chaos of tight deadlines and breaking news. These professionals often function in high-stress circumstances, necessitating supportive networks to keep spirits aloft and integrity intact. When surrounded by colleagues who inspire and challenge them to think differently, journalists can more easily embrace current experiences with clarity and purpose.

Returning to the professional field at large, the presence of a mentor can serve as an invaluable influence. Mentors offer not only guidance but also reassurance, helping individuals to navigate through complex situations without succumbing to imagined fears. Their insights into balancing personal and professional hurdles empower mentees to remain grounded, reinforcing the importance of engaging fully with the present.

Yet, even with exemplary role models and peers, it is ultimately up to each person to choose how they interact with their immediate surroundings. Mindfulness and active reflection on daily experiences can help regulate the focus on the present. For performers in entertainment, practicing mindfulness may involve being fully aware during rehearsals, allowing them to deliver more authentic performances onstage. Similarly, for a marketing executive, taking mindful breaks throughout the day can dispel undue stress, paving the way for clearer thinking and effective decision-making.

By creating space to truly see and appraise each moment, we open ourselves to life's nuances. The beauty lies not in control, but in participation—watching, engaging, and evolving. The cliché rings true: Yesterday is history, tomorrow is a mystery, today is a gift—that's why it's called the present. While anticipation and planning hold their place, they must never eclipse our current reality, lest we fall prey to the illusory troubles our mind conjures.

Belief and Its Impact on Present Living

Belief acts as a bridge between the difficulties we face today and the hope for brighter tomorrows. This belief, that tomorrow can indeed be better, eases the weight of present challenges. It's akin to having a lighthouse guiding us through the tempestuous seas of work-life uncertainty. A simple reassurance that things will improve can alleviate stress, letting us find solace amid chaos.

Consider a sales professional facing dwindling quarterly results due to market shifts; instead of panicking, their belief in turning things around sparks creativity and diligence. They'll brainstorm fresh strategies, perhaps tapping into untapped networks or tweaking their marketing pitches. Such proactive approaches stem from the conviction that today's setbacks are mere stepping stones to tomorrow's triumphs. This mindset fosters resilience, making difficult times more bearable and encouraging persistence until success is achieved.

Similarly, viewing our past positively aids in enduring today's difficulties. The narratives we build around past experiences significantly shape our current outlook. Reframing past events as learning opportunities rather than failures primes us for growth. In high-pressure fields like media and journalism or management, reflecting on past challenges with a constructive lens provides invaluable lessons. By understanding mistakes as part of our journey, we enrich ourselves with insights and become better equipped to handle present adversities.

Take, for example, an athlete who missed a crucial goal in a significant match. If they view this setback merely as a failure, it might haunt their future performances. However, if approached constructively, considering what they learned from that experience, such as improving focus under pressure or enhancing technical skills, they pave the way for future successes. Each misstep becomes a stepping stone, transforming adversity into opportunity.

This positive reframing can translate into everyday life too. Imagine a marketing specialist who once led a failed campaign. Instead of dwelling on the missed targets, they retrace their steps, understand what didn't work, and adapt these findings to refine future campaigns. Learning from the past doesn't mean obsessing over it but using it as a foundation to build a stronger, more resilient present.

Focusing on the present moment is essential for achieving personal wellness and reaching goals. When immersed in the chaos of impending deadlines or competitive rivalries, it's easy to get lost in the noise of what-ifs and hypotheticals. Yet, grounding oneself in the present circumvents this anxiety-laden distraction. Emphasizing mindfulness prevents energy drains caused by speculative worries about the future or regrets about the past.

In the realm of advertising, where trends shift rapidly, staying present allows marketers to respond agilely to consumer needs.

Instead of fixating on a future trend that may or may not materialize, they concentrate on the current audience's feedback and demand, crafting advertisements that resonate authentically. This adaptability keeps them at the forefront of industry evolution, constantly innovating and connecting with the audience meaningfully.

Similarly, management professionals benefit immensely from present-focus strategies. By concentrating on immediate tasks and managerial decisions, they foster a productive environment that nurtures team growth and operational efficiency. Overthinking potential hurdles down the line only distracts from effectively managing today's resources and challenges.

The mantra "If I can look up, I can get up!" captures the essence of this approach. When grounded in the present while maintaining hopeful optimism for the future, resilience becomes second nature. Professionals across diverse sectors thrive when they internalize this balance, enabling them to navigate both foreseeable and unforeseeable challenges adeptly.

Furthermore, living in the present encourages authentic connections. In professions such as sports and entertainment, being truly present during engagements—whether training sessions, rehearsals, or live performances—enhances the quality of those experiences. Performers who remain attentive to their craft in real time deliver genuine artistry, captivating audiences worldwide.

However, staying present doesn't imply ignoring future aspirations or past lessons; it means acknowledging their influence while prioritizing now. In entrepreneurship, this translates to focusing on current business operations while setting visionary yet realistic goals. Entrepreneurs must learn from previous ventures' outcomes and strategize for future growth, all while prioritizing current tasks to sustain momentum.

This intricate dance between past, present, and future requires nuanced understanding. By keeping belief central to this juggling act, professionals find harmony amid challenging landscapes. The persistent focus on now, punctuated with faith in better tomorrows and appreciation for past experiences, invigorates the pursuit of goals.

The optimism inherent in believing in change empowers individuals to translate it into actionable steps toward progress. As belief aligns with purposeful actions rooted in the present, it manifests tangible results, ultimately achieving personal and professional fulfillment. Through this lens, daily adversities become manageable, infusing everyday grind with purpose and direction.

Final Insights

In this chapter, we delved into the essential practice of living in the present while managing our worries about the future. Professionals often find themselves torn between past successes and future uncertainties, but the key lies in focusing on what can be done now. By embracing the present, we open ourselves to opportunities that otherwise might be overshadowed by undue concerns. We all want to be successful. But success doesn't live in the past, and it doesn't wait in the future. It's built in the micro-moments we often overlook—the daily decisions, the present commitments, the hard conversations we don't put off. It's easy to fall into the trap of living in memories or projections. But both can become distractions if they're not anchored in action.

In this chapter, we explored how living in the present is more than a feel-good mantra—it's a competitive advantage. It's how you stay resilient under pressure. It's how you keep showing up when the outcome is still uncertain. Whether you're leading a team, running a business, or chasing a personal goal, your future won't be built on what you're hoping will happen. It'll be built on what you do today.

We saw how one young athlete, Sara, let commitment—not circumstance—shape her path. We contrasted that with stories of people who were too focused on what had already happened or what might happen, and in the process missed the opportunity to grow now.

Because that's the thing about the present: It's not just where life happens. It's where growth happens. It's where confidence is built, trust is earned, and progress is made.

And sometimes, the moment that turns everything around doesn't look like a breakthrough—it looks like lying on the floor, watching *Rocky*. It looks like someone shouting, "Get up!" when everything in you wants to stay down. But if you hear that voice—and act on it—you start the comeback. You stop being defined by what happened and start defining what happens next.

Guidelines

- Energy is best invested in the present. The past is a lesson. The future is a possibility. But the now is a gift.
- Have faith that the seeds you plant today will bloom in time. Stop forecasting failure and start acting with intention.
- Life is unpredictable. Stay grounded in your values and adaptable in your actions.

Takeaways

- Success is built in micro-moments.
- Worry is energy with no ROI.
- The present is where the future gets made.
- The only real power you have is what you do now.

Ask Yourself

- Am I spending more time worrying about the future than acting on what I can control today?
- What's one small step I can take right now that aligns with my bigger vision?
- Do my daily habits reflect the person I want to become?

When you learn to stay where your feet are, everything changes. You make better decisions. You show up more fully. And slowly, day by day, you become the kind of person your future was waiting for.

Just like Rocky—beaten, bloodied, and told to stay down—you get up.

And that's when everything begins to shift.

Chapter 7

WHERE'S THAT DICK GOING?

Relativity of the Future

The most impactful, well-crafted sports film I've ever seen is *Miracle*. It's not just a story about hockey. It's a blueprint for belief. It tells the story of Herb Brooks and the 1980 US Olympic hockey team—a group of college kids and amateur athletes who had no business even being on the ice with the Soviets, let alone dreaming of gold.

These weren't seasoned teammates. They were rivals. In some cases, enemies. But Herb Brooks saw something no one else could. Not the press. Not the fans. Not even the players themselves. He believed in the power of unity—and in the alchemy that happens when you combine raw skill with discipline and bind it all together with shared purpose.

At the time, the Soviets were unstoppable. They hadn't lost in nearly 20 years. In a warm-up game, they crushed Team USA 11–3. But belief doesn't live in the past. It lives in the present—aimed at the future.

Herb's genius wasn't just in coaching. It was in how he made belief contagious. He didn't just train hockey players. He aligned energy. He created collective consciousness. And in doing so, he gave his team permission to outgrow their limitations.

The real miracle wasn't beating the Russians. It was resetting after that emotional high and finishing the job against Sweden to win gold. That's the relativity of the future. When no one else believes in you, when they laugh at your vision, when they scoff at your goals—that's when belief becomes your superpower. Stay aligned with that vision long enough, and the doubters will be the ones applauding.

Herb Brooks didn't just build a hockey team. He built a living, breathing example of what happens when belief, purpose, and preparation collide in the present moment to create timeless impact.

Understanding the *relativity of the future* means recognizing that our beliefs about what's ahead shape how we show up right now. Each image we hold in our mind—each possibility we allow ourselves to imagine—becomes a blueprint for the reality we create.

Our imagination is more than daydreaming. It's a neurological superpower. Neuroscience tells us that the brain often doesn't distinguish between vividly imagined events and real ones. Athletes visualize performance to increase accuracy. Public speakers rehearse mentally before stepping onstage. Entrepreneurs picture successful outcomes to boost confidence and resilience. What we imagine, we begin to embody.

But imagination is only half the equation. The other half is *alignment*—making sure our daily energy and actions match the future we say we want. This is where the idea of "vibrational relativity" comes into play—not as self-help fluff, but as practical physics. Everything in the universe vibrates. From subatomic particles to entire ecosystems, everything moves, resonates, and interacts.

What makes humans extraordinary is that we can *consciously* shift our frequency. Gratitude can elevate our state. Stress can drag it down. Vision can pull us forward. Emotion, thought, and intention don't just reflect our energy—they direct it.

To say you're "raising your vibration" isn't about floating away on a cloud—it's about anchoring into a mindset and an emotional state that supports the future you're building. It's about tuning your internal frequency to the outcomes you want to attract.

When Herb Brooks aligned that team—not just strategically, but energetically—he wasn't just coaching. He was conducting.

This chapter will guide you through how to harness that same principle in your own work and life. Whether you're leading a team, launching a startup, or stepping into a new chapter of your personal life, the future isn't something that happens *to* you. It's something that takes shape *through* you.

By the end of this chapter, you'll understand how to:

- Use imagination as a strategy tool, not just an escape hatch.
- Align daily habits with long-term visions.
- Shift your energy toward belief, even when the scoreboard says otherwise.

Because the truth is, your future isn't written. It's vibrationally invited. And belief? That's the invitation.

Vibrations and Imagination

In the grand orchestra of life, every entity vibrates at its own unique frequency. This isn't just poetic metaphor—it's scientific fact. According to quantum physics, even the objects that appear solid and still are composed of atoms in constant motion. From subatomic particles to planetary bodies, everything resonates with energy. We live in a universe defined by vibration.

But here is where humans are extraordinary: We don't just vibrate. We can consciously raise our vibration. Unlike other beings, we have the capacity to shift our energetic state through thought, emotion, intention, and imagination. That's the true gift. We can use gratitude to lift our frequency. We can use forgiveness to clear emotional static. And we can use vision to create realities that don't yet exist.

To vibrate with a unique frequency isn't about being esoteric—it's about living in alignment with your values, your truth, your purpose. When you do, your energy doesn't just attract the right opportunities—it amplifies them. That's how visionaries pull future possibility into present momentum. That's how leaders magnetize movements. That's how creators birth what didn't exist yesterday into what everyone sees tomorrow.

Imagination is the engine of this vibration. It's what sets humans apart from every other species. Animals survive by reacting to their environment. Humans thrive by imagining something better. While a dog may whine or pace when left alone, reflecting learned behavior and emotional distress, it doesn't sit and picture a better version of its afternoon. It doesn't envision how it might build a staircase to open the door.

But we do. We imagine businesses before they exist. We write songs before they're ever sung. We architect cities, revolutions, and solutions—first in the mind, then in reality. That's imagination's power. It doesn't just entertain; it generates. It vibrates at the frequency of potential.

Reason is essential—it helps us navigate the present. But imagination? That's what builds the bridge to the future. Reason will get you through the maze. Imagination will let you invent a whole new path.

And here's the part that matters most: Your imagination already knows the way. If you allow it space. If you give it permission. If you stop talking yourself out of what you haven't even tried yet. The ability to see what doesn't yet exist and move toward it anyway is a competitive edge. It's not just a nice-to-have. It's a survival skill.

So how do you start? Create environments that welcome imagination. Schedule brainstorms with no judgment. Keep a vision journal. Say "what if?" more often. Surround yourself with ideas, art, music, questions, and people who stretch your perspective. Every time you imagine a different future, you raise your vibration—and move one step closer to making it real.

The truth is that your imagination is already working. It's already picturing something. The only question is: Are you aiming it where you want to go?

Overcoming Fear

In a fast-paced world where decisions are made in the blink of an eye, fear often emerges as a shadowy figure, fabricating barriers that seem insurmountable. Yet, at its core, fear is largely a construct—a product of our rapid thought processes and self-constructed perceptions. It often masquerades as reality when, in truth, it has no more substance than a fleeting nightmare upon waking.

Our minds operate with incredible speed, assessing threats and making snap judgments in milliseconds. While this ability is beneficial for immediate survival, it can build unnecessary defenses in our professional and personal lives. In competitive environments like sales or marketing, the perceived threat of failure can loom large. These fears, although unfounded, can paralyze creative thinking and stifle innovation. They prompt us to erect defenses against challenges that exist only in our imaginations, hampering our potential for growth.

The journey to understanding fear as an illusion begins with recognizing how we unconsciously engage in these defensive mechanisms. Many professionals navigate their careers with caution, constantly evaluating risks and rewards. This hypersensitivity, driven by imagined outcomes, often leads to missed opportunities. For instance, a marketing executive may hesitate to pitch a groundbreaking idea, fearing rejection or criticism. In reality, this hesitation stems from an imaginary scenario within, rather than any external truth.

However, dismantling these fears is possible through an intentional embrace of truth over illusion. By accepting that many fears are simply constructs of the mind, we can pave the way for genuine progress. This acceptance requires a shift in perspective, challenging the narratives we've built around what is considered threatening. As we strip away these layers of illusion, we make space for clarity and focus, essential components in achieving future goals.

Living a life rooted in truth involves deliberate practice. It is about acknowledging uncertainties without letting them dictate our actions. When we let go of the facades of fear, our vibrational state enhances, aligning us with higher energies that promote positivity and courage. For example, an entrepreneur might once have feared the unpredictability of launching a new venture. But by focusing on the truth of their capabilities and the value of their innovations, they channel energy into creation rather than apprehension.

Consider a sports coach who encourages players to face formidable opponents not with dread but with the belief in their training and team support. Accepting the truth—their skills, preparation, and teamwork—over the illusion of invincibility in the opponent transforms the game. Similarly, embracing truth in professional settings liberates teams to explore innovative solutions without the constraints of fear-induced limitations.

Maintaining this state of clarity demands continuous effort but yields exponential benefits. Intentional practice in seeking truth over illusion minimizes the impact of fear on decision-making and goal achievement. It cultivates an environment where imagination flourishes unencumbered by restrictive thoughts, enabling professionals to chart paths that were previously deemed unreachable.

In environments rife with competition, from advertising to entrepreneurship, the power lies in harnessing the truth of our vision. Believing in the truth of our dreams shapes the future, as intention coupled with authenticity can push the boundaries of what is possible. Professionals across industries benefit greatly from internalizing this mindset, allowing innovation to thrive in spaces where fear once reigned.

Beliefs and Limitations

Understanding how our beliefs and perceived limitations shape the future is pivotal to living within the values we want to embody. I've always sought to begin by focusing on dreams and possibilities rather than obstacles. While the dreams don't always win, belief alone can help steer us toward a powerful positive future. When individuals envision what they aspire to achieve without being bogged down by hurdles, their mindset shifts toward optimism and creativity. This shift in perspective is not just about wishful thinking; it's an intentional realignment of focus that encourages growth and innovation.

Consider the story of Thomas Edison, who famously stated, "I have not failed. I've just found 10,000 ways that won't work." His relentless pursuit of invention wasn't hindered by failures or perceived limits but was driven by the potent belief in his dream of creating the electric light bulb. Such historical examples remind us that when we focus on overcoming barriers and maintain our belief in the possible, the future unfolds with renewed promise.

Einstein's views on technological advancements serve as a sober reminder of the need for foresight. He cautioned against the unrestrained development of technologies that could potentially surpass ethical considerations and lead to destruction rather than progress. Einstein's concerns were not unfounded. Technological innovations have, at times, outpaced our moral and ethical frameworks, leading to unintended consequences. Nuclear energy, while a significant leap in technology, also birthed nuclear weapons, raising questions about humanity's ability to responsibly manage such power.

This warning emphasizes the necessity of maintaining balance as we innovate. The idea of technological regression underscores this need for caution—reminding society that unchecked progress may not always benefit future generations. It prompts us to reassess how we approach advancements, ensuring that considerations of safety, sustainability, and ethics are integrated into the development process. This balanced approach ensures that we do not lose sight of long-term impacts while striving for immediate gains.

On the flip side, believing in the constructive power of dreams facilitates innovation and collective advancement. Dreams are not merely whimsical pursuits; they are foundational to transformative ideas and breakthroughs. Steve Jobs's belief in the potential of personal computers revolutionized global communication and business operations. His vision turned Apple into one of the most influential companies worldwide, showing how a steadfast belief in possibilities can ripple through industries and communities.

Moreover, when people believe collectively in shared dreams, there is a synergistic effect that amplifies their potential to drive change. Communities and organizations that foster an environment where innovative ideas are encouraged often witness extraordinary outcomes. This collective belief creates a dynamic where individuals are motivated to contribute their best efforts, leading to remarkable achievements that might otherwise seem unattainable.

Guidelines for living life as if it's the last time experiencing it become crucial here. This mindset propels individuals to take action, seize opportunities, and embrace challenges with vigor. It instills urgency and a sense of purpose, compelling people to make the most of their experiences and contributions. By continually striving to be our higher selves, we enhance our capabilities and broaden our impact on shaping a better future.

Living in the Present

Embracing the present moment can be both a challenge and a gift. This journey begins with recognizing that each experience is distinct, offering opportunities for growth, reflection, and engagement that might otherwise pass unnoticed. By treating every moment as unique, we cultivate a greater appreciation for what's before us, allowing us to spot opportunities that could shape our future. For instance, those moments of spontaneity in a busy workday or an unexpected conversation during a networking event could open doors to new collaborations or ideas.

Imagine the power of living each day with awareness and

gratitude. When we consciously appreciate the details—a colleague's insight, a project's challenge, or a task well done—we elevate our vibrational state. This heightened awareness doesn't just fill our days with purpose; it sets the tone for what's to come. In this elevated state, intuition becomes sharper, decisions more aligned, and creativity boundless, amplifying our potential to envision and manifest a promising future.

Trusting in an unknown yet benevolent future is crucial in navigating life's uncertainties. While it's natural to feel apprehensive about what lies ahead, faith in positive outcomes aligns us with higher vibrational states. Embracing this trust means acknowledging that, while we can't control every aspect of what will happen, we have the power to choose our perspective and responses. Consider the story of entrepreneurs who venture into uncharted territories; their belief in a favorable outcome propels them toward innovation and success, even when the path seems unclear.

This mindset encourages resilience and adaptability, both essential qualities in today's competitive environments. Viewing the future as a landscape filled with possibilities rather than obstacles shifts our focus from fear to opportunity. Professionals who maintain this optimistic outlook often report feeling empowered and motivated, ready to seize whatever comes their way. Aligning ourselves with these higher vibrations not only enhances personal development but also positions us to be proactive architects of our futures.

Parallel to dreaming of the future is the importance of self-acceptance and love. Striving for improvement should never overshadow the need for self-compassion. Balancing ambition with kindness toward oneself creates a fertile ground for both personal and spiritual growth. Consider the individual who is constantly setting high expectations in their career; without self-love, the relentless pursuit of goals can lead to burnout. However, when balanced with self-care and understanding, this drive transforms into a journey of enlightenment and fulfillment.

Self-improvement and self-love are not mutually exclusive. They complement each other, creating a dynamic push and pull that keeps us grounded while reaching for the stars. By nurturing our well-being, we build resilience against setbacks and foster a mindset that welcomes growth. Stories abound of leaders who attribute their success not only to their skills but to their ability to forgive their missteps and learn from them. This harmony between striving and self-kindness paves the way for deeper satisfaction and clearer vision as we advance.

As we look to the future, it becomes evident that building prospects collectively yields the greatest rewards. The idea that we cannot construct the future for just ourselves is pivotal. Unity, collaboration, and shared success lay the foundation for a more inclusive and prosperous tomorrow. From marketing teams brainstorming innovative campaigns to athletes working together for a common goal, the synergy of united efforts challenges the status quo and achieves extraordinary results.

To walk with dreamers and believers is to harness the collective power of diverse perspectives and aspirations. Collaborations thrive on the energy and ideas everyone brings to the table, elevating projects beyond individual capabilities. Shared experiences unite us, fostering a culture of mutual support and encouragement. When professionals co-create, they not only achieve remarkable milestones but also forge enduring connections that extend beyond the immediate task at hand.

Let inspiration ignite a fire within us, serving as a catalyst for action and transformation. Inspiration can stem from witnessing others' achievements, learning from their journeys, or simply sharing in their dreams. It becomes the driving force that propels us toward realizing our full potential, both individually and collectively. By encouraging each other to dream big and aim high, we create a ripple effect that inspires more people to pursue their aspirations, ultimately leading to a richer and more vibrant future.

Optimism and Vision

When I talk about the relativity of the future, I don't just mean time in a calendar sense. I'm talking about how we shape our future by the meaning we assign to our past and the faith we bring into the present. The truth is the future isn't fixed. It's flexible. It's molded by our mindset, by how productively we act, how positively we perceive, and how purposefully we live in this exact moment.

That is where gratitude, which we've looked at throughout the book in different ways, again surfaces. Gratitude is the tool that tunes us to the frequency of abundance. When we seek the light, the love, and the lessons in everything, especially the challenges, we shift our perception of what is possible. And when we forgive, not just others but also ourselves, and even what we think others think about us, that is when real optimism kicks in.

Now, I've always been an optimist. I've even jokingly called myself the "top optimist." But let me be real with you. I didn't come up with that mindset on my own. I had a teacher. My grandfather Papa Goldberg. We didn't call him the top optimist. We called him the poptimist.

That man could find the light in a blackout. He was the Viktor Frankl of our family. No matter what life threw his way, he found meaning. He found joy. He found purpose. You could hand him a pile of problems, and he would somehow turn it into a pathway.

The way I see it, optimism is inherited not by blood, but by example. And if I'm the top optimist, it's only because I had the privilege of learning from the greatest poptimist of all time.

Personal stories of resilience often highlight the transformative power of maintaining a positive outlook even when faced with adversity. In challenging times, such as economic downturns or organizational setbacks, individuals who focus on staying hopeful tend to emerge stronger. Their optimism acts as a beacon, guiding them through uncertainty and helping them see opportunities where others might see obstacles. This mindset not only enhances their own prospects but also inspires those around them to strive for betterment. When we reflect on such stories, it becomes evident that positivity has the potential to shift perceptions, enabling people to overcome challenges and conceive a brighter future.

Exemplary leaders like Herb Brooks illustrate how vision can be transformed into tangible success. Brooks's ability to articulate a clear and inspiring goal fueled his team's determination and dedication. The Miracle on Ice, as the team's victory over the Soviet Union came to be known, serves as a testament to the power of vision in achieving what seems impossible. Brooks's strategy was not just about tactics on the ice; it was about instilling a belief in possibilities and galvanizing his players to reach beyond what they thought possible.

The Miracle on Ice epitomizes how belief in possibility can surmount formidable challenges. Against all odds, the US team's triumph became a symbol of hope, demonstrating that unwavering belief can defy expectations and create profound moments of achievement. The players, inspired by their coach's vision, cultivated a strong sense of belief and commitment, which fueled their performance. Their journey from underdogs to champions underscores the importance of faith in your abilities and the pursuit of excellence, even when the odds seem insurmountable.

Moreover, collective belief and motivation can inspire individuals to pursue miracles and achieve greatness. In any organization or team, when members share a common purpose and align their efforts toward a collective goal, the results can be extraordinary. For example, a sales team facing high targets might initially perceive them as unattainable. However, by cultivating a shared vision and maintaining a positive atmosphere, they can transform these targets into stepping stones toward success. The synergy created by unified belief generates momentum, propelling the group forward and reinforcing individual contributions.

To foster such an atmosphere, it's essential to integrate strategies that leverage optimism as a vehicle for building a better future. Here, we can take inspiration from "Papa's optimism as a strategy for a better future." By envisioning success and adopting a hopeful attitude, individuals can manifest change and guide themselves toward desired outcomes. A guideline for integrating optimism involves practicing gratitude, setting positive intentions, and visualizing success regularly. These practices empower individuals to maintain a good vibrational state, fostering creativity, problem-solving, and resilience.

Similarly, examining how "Herb Brooks motivated his team through belief in miracles" provides valuable insights. Leaders can utilize optimism as a tool to cultivate belief within their teams. By encouraging a mindset that embraces challenges as opportunities for learning and growth, leaders can inspire confidence and drive. Creating an environment where team members feel supported and valued further enhances collective motivation, boosting the likelihood of achieving ambitious goals.

Final Insights

As we've explored in this chapter, the relativity of the future isn't just about time—it's about energy. It's about how imagination, belief, and intention shape the path ahead. When we align our thoughts with purpose and gratitude, we don't just forecast a better future— we start building it, moment by moment, from the inside out.

Vibrational relativity reminds us that we don't passively arrive at our destiny—we tune in to it. Through imagination, we become architects of possibility. Through belief, we gain the courage to act. And through purpose, we calibrate the energy we carry and the impact we make. In business, in sport, in art, in life—those who move forward most powerfully are often those who imagined it first.

Guidelines

- Before you build, calibrate. Begin with quiet. Get clear on what you want— not just what the world wants from you.
- Use your imagination as a design tool. Visualize the life, project, or outcome you want in sharp, emotional detail. Where are you? Who are you with? How do you feel?
- Behave like the future is already happening. Speak, act, and decide as if your vision is real—because every decision you make today is casting a vote for that version of tomorrow.
- Let gratitude, forgiveness, and joy raise your energy. Low vibration states like fear, shame, or bitterness can distort your signal. Clear the static to stay aligned.
- Energy is contagious. Choose people, ideas, and environments that reflect belief and expansion—not contraction or doubt.

Takeaways

- The future is flexible—shaped by belief, not just circumstance.
- Your imagination is more than a dream—it's a neurological tool.
- Action aligned with intention becomes momentum.
- Fear is often a mirage—truth is the better compass.
- When you live in purpose, you don't chase the future. You attract it.

Ask Yourself

- What future am I imagining for myself right now?
- Are my habits and energy aligned with that vision?
- Am I surrounding myself with people who elevate or drain my belief?
- What fear or illusion might be distorting my direction?
- What's one bold, imaginative action I can take today to invite that future closer?

When I was younger, I thought optimism was personality. Now I know it's practice.

Belief is not wishful thinking. It's directional energy. It's the mindset that lets us reset after failure, keep going when no one else believes, and stay the course when the payoff is still out of sight. The future is flexible. And it's listening.

So here's your invitation: Be your own poptimist. Choose belief over fear. Vision over cynicism. Imagination over limitation.

Because the future is listening.

And it's waiting to hear what you believe next.

PART 3

LIVING THE FOUR GREAT TRUTHS

Chapter 8

I'M SORRY, DICK

Practice Empathy and
Surround Yourself with Forgiveness

Navigating the professional world can often feel like a complex dance of competition and collaboration, where maintaining relationships becomes as important as achieving targets. In such an environment, misunderstandings and breaches of trust are not uncommon, making forgiveness a valuable skill to cultivate. Forgiveness is more than just an act of kindness or a way to mend fences; it's a powerful tool that can transform both personal and professional lives. Letting go of past grievances allows individuals to move forward with clarity and a renewed sense of purpose. When we forgive, we release ourselves from the burdens of anger and resentment, clearing a path for growth and positive change. It enables us to see beyond immediate conflicts and fosters a mindset open to possibilities rather than dwelling on setbacks.

This chapter delves into the essence of surrounding oneself with forgiveness, exploring how it can impact not only our perception of sin but also our interactions in high-pressure environments. We'll uncover the role of forgiveness in fostering empathy and understanding, which are crucial for cultivating productive and harmonious workplaces. By examining real-life examples and narratives, you'll discover how self-forgiveness serves as the foundation for extending authentic forgiveness to others. This chapter also offers practical insights into nurturing a forgiving mindset, highlighting its importance in leadership and community-building within competitive fields. Whether you're leading a team in marketing or facing the pressures of entrepreneurship, embracing forgiveness can pave the way for stronger, more compassionate relationships and unlock potential pathways toward success.

Over the years, I've had the honor of coaching professional athletes, many of them during a vulnerable chapter of their lives—toward the end of their careers or in that often disorienting time after retirement. It's during those moments that the biggest battles are no longer physical. They're internal. Mental. Emotional. Spiritual.

One athlete in particular stands out. A talented baseball player who once wore the uniform of the San Diego Padres. On the field, he had the skills. But off the field, he was grappling with something far more powerful than any pitch or swing: addiction. The drugs were one thing, but the real weight came from the guilt and shame that followed. He was stuck in a loop of resentment, anger, anxiety, and regret—not just about what he had done, but about how others perceived him. And worse, how he thought they perceived him.

He couldn't stop worrying about what people thought, or what he thought they thought about him. I see it all the time. When our ego traps us in the judgments of others—real or imagined—it becomes nearly impossible to move forward.

But something began to shift the moment he embraced humility—not as weakness, but as strength. He stopped trying to defend himself. He stopped rewriting the past. And he started forgiving himself. Truly. Deeply. Completely.

That forgiveness unlocked something. It brought him peace. Not because the world suddenly changed—but because he did. With that inner shift came clarity. And with clarity came purpose.

He made a comeback, not just in baseball, but in life. And when the time came to hang up his cleats, he didn't retreat from the spotlight—he stepped into it. He spoke at Boys & Girls Clubs, walked into elementary schools, shared his story with courage and vulnerability. He knew his struggles weren't just a burden—they were a bridge. A way to help others avoid the same pain. He turned his dummy tax into a deposit of wisdom for the next generation.

That's the power of humility. That's the freedom of forgiveness. It saved his life. And I have no doubt it's gone on to save many others.

And that's where we begin this chapter.

Forgiveness and empathy are more than just soft skills. They're powerful levers that can transform both personal and professional lives. Letting go of past grievances allows us to move forward with clarity and renewed purpose. When we forgive, we release ourselves from the burdens of resentment and regret—and that opens up space. For creativity. For empathy. For connection.

In this chapter, as we move into how we can better live according to our Four Great Truths that have shaped every relationship I build—empathy and forgiveness, gratitude, accountability, and effective communication—we'll start by exploring how to cultivate a forgiving mindset and why it's so critical to surround yourself with people who practice that too. We'll dig into how self-forgiveness becomes the foundation for forgiving others, and how both open the door to empathy—the kind of empathy that makes relationships more resilient and leadership more human. Whether you're leading a team in marketing or navigating the pressures of high-stakes entrepreneurship, empathy and forgiveness are two of the strongest tools you've got. Let's put them to work.

The Nature of Forgiveness

Let's be honest—forgiveness is hard. Especially in a world where we're taught to define ourselves and others by wins and losses, right and wrong. We carry around guilt for the things we've done, resentment for what's been done to us, and shame for the gap between who we are and who we thought we'd be. But here's the truth: Forgiveness isn't really about the other person.

It's about freeing ourselves.

We've all heard the word "sin" thrown around, but here's a perspective that's emerged for me through years of coaching and personal spiritual work: Sin isn't just about morality, religion, or judgment. It's about misalignment. Sin is what happens when we forget who we are and start operating from fear, scarcity, ego, or resentment.

Forgiveness, then, is the correction. It's the conscious choice to return to alignment. To remember our light. To stop punishing ourselves or others for being human. And when we view it that way, forgiveness stops being passive—it becomes powerful.

It doesn't mean forgetting. It doesn't mean excusing. It means choosing peace over pain. Growth over grudges. Alignment over ego. Before we can ever hope to forgive others, we have to learn how to forgive ourselves. That's where real healing begins.

Think about it. Just like on an airplane, you're told to secure your own oxygen mask before helping someone else. Forgiveness works the same way. You can't give what you don't have. You can't pour from an empty cup. And you certainly can't offer grace to others if you're still holding yourself hostage to guilt, shame, or regret.

In the rhythm of professional life, it's easy to carry the weight of past mistakes—missed opportunities, poor decisions, relationships we mishandled, or moments when fear got the best of us. We beat ourselves up quietly, thinking it's the price of getting better. But that kind of punishment doesn't lead to growth. It just lowers your frequency and traps you in the past.

Self-forgiveness isn't about letting yourself off the hook. It's about accepting your humanness. It's recognizing that growth comes from learning—and learning often comes from falling short. When you release the need to be perfect, you create space for real progress.

Only when we free ourselves from internal criticism can we connect authentically with others and extend that same forgiveness outward. That's when relationships deepen, leadership evolves, and compassion expands.

Self-forgiveness isn't selfish. It's foundational. It's the first step to living in alignment, serving at your highest capacity, and showing up with a heart that's open, not guarded.

Take Emma, a project manager in a high-stress marketing firm. She had always been her harshest critic. Her inability to forgive herself for past mistakes made it nearly impossible to forgive her team when they fell short. But once she started practicing self-forgiveness—really letting go of the old internal blame—everything changed. Her relationships with her colleagues improved. The team became more cohesive, more open. That shift didn't start with them. It started with her.

Because here's the thing: The power of forgiveness doesn't just lighten the load—it illuminates the illusion that we're broken. It reveals that sin isn't a permanent stain. It's a human experience. One that teaches. One that transforms.

Without self-forgiveness, it's nearly impossible to offer the real thing to others. Holding on to internal resentment narrows our bandwidth for empathy. In competitive environments, that creates more friction than flow. It breeds tension instead of trust.

But leaders who model self-forgiveness? They unlock something in the people around them. They normalize imperfection. They show what grace in motion looks like. And that softens a team's shoulders. That raises morale. That creates an environment where people feel safe enough to try, fail, and try again.

So how do we begin? Start with quiet introspection. Name the guilt or regret you're carrying. Don't judge it—just name it. Then, reflect on what it's taught you. And from there, release it. Speak it out loud. Write it down. Burn it if you have to. The progression is simple: Acknowledge. Reflect. Forgive.

You cannot offer what you do not possess. If you want to forgive others freely, you must forgive yourself first.

Imagine what would happen if entire industries took this to heart. What if marketing agencies, startups, or sales teams became places where mistakes weren't fatal—but foundational? What if leaders stopped using shame as a motivator and started using forgiveness as a multiplier?

That's how culture shifts. That's how industries evolve. Not just through strategy or performance—but through people who have done the inner work, and who lead from a place of empathy, understanding, and grace.

And it all starts here: I'm sorry. I forgive you. I forgive me.

The Power of Forgiveness

Forgiveness is more than just a personal act; it's a transformative journey that can profoundly impact both individuals and communities. In our fast-paced, competitive worlds, understanding this power is crucial for fostering harmony. When we talk about forgiveness, the first thing that comes to mind is the inner peace it brings by replacing hatred and vengeance with understanding. This isn't just a personal belief but a reality observed in various situations across the globe.

Take, for instance, the remarkable response of some families to the 2015 Charleston church shooting in South Carolina. Amid unimaginable grief, they chose to forgive the shooter. The world watched as these families expressed compassion instead of seeking revenge. This brave choice not only illustrated immense strength but also sent a powerful message of unity and healing. It demonstrated how forgiveness could transcend personal pain, setting an example of love triumphing over hate.

This act of forgiveness doesn't imply forgetting or dismissing the wrongdoing. Instead, it represents a conscious decision to let go of bitterness and resentment, which often consume us from within. By choosing to forgive, we allow ourselves to replace anger with empathy, creating fertile ground for growth and reconciliation. As individuals learn to forgive, they find themselves less burdened by the emotional weight of grudges, resulting in a clearer, more focused mindset ready to tackle life's myriad challenges.

Moreover, forgiveness enhances resilience against life's inevitable ups and downs. In a professional setting, where stress is rampant and pressures run high, holding on to grievances only adds layers of unnecessary complexity. By embracing forgiveness, we improve our capacity to bounce back from setbacks, turning potential roadblocks into stepping stones toward success. Inner peace, promoted by forgiveness, becomes the secret weapon we wield to navigate through turbulent times with grace and poise.

The ripple effect of forgiveness doesn't stop at the individual level. Its influence extends to communities, encouraging a culture of mutual respect and cooperation. When members of a community choose to forgive, they collectively move toward a state of harmony. This collective goodness fuels the community's progress, making it more resilient and versatile in confronting social issues. Forgiveness fosters environments where collaboration thrives over competition, transforming workplaces into supportive spaces that nurture creativity and innovation.

As we continue exploring the power of forgiveness, it's important to acknowledge the journey it entails. Forgiving is not instantaneous; it requires patience and effort. Yet, once embraced, it pulls us closer to a state of harmony with ourselves and others. This sense of togetherness cultivates a shared understanding and purpose, guiding communities toward collective goals and aspirations.

Ultimately, the true beauty of forgiveness lies in its cyclical nature. When we forgive, we set off a chain reaction inspiring others to do the same. A forgiving mindset attracts similar energies, drawing people toward positivity and support. In an environment marked by forgiveness, relationships flourish, trust deepens, and conflicts resolve more easily, reinforcing the foundation of any thriving society or workplace.

Misconceptions About Forgiveness

Forgiveness is often misunderstood as an undeserved gift or a denial of the truth. Some see it as a free pass for someone who does not deserve it. Others mistake it for pretending the pain never happened.

But forgiveness isn't about excusing the behavior or denying the truth; it's about freeing yourself from the emotional prison the experience has created. You are not letting them off the hook. You are letting yourself off the hook. You are releasing the grip the pain has on your peace, so you can move forward with clarity, not bitterness.

Forgiveness does not erase the past. It reclaims your future.

Imagine for a moment that the grudge you hold is like carrying a heavy backpack filled with stones. Each stone represents pain, betrayal, and bitterness. Over time, this weight becomes exhausting and may even prevent you from enjoying life's moments. Forgiveness allows us to put down the backpack, feeling lighter and more at ease. By choosing to forgive, we allow ourselves to breathe deeper and appreciate the present without the shadow of past grievances.

While some view forgiveness skeptically, equating it with weakness or naivete, it actually requires great strength and willpower. Choosing to forgive is an act of courage, demanding self-reflection and empathy. This perspective helps dispel any notion that forgiveness is merely an easy way out. Instead, it represents one of the most significant steps in personal development and emotional resilience. It's a powerful choice to let go of what no longer serves us and make room for healing and growth.

One critical aspect of forgiveness is understanding its relationship with guilt. Holding on to guilt perpetuates suffering, while forgiveness offers a pathway to release. Guilt can serve as a reminder of our imperfections, constantly replaying scenarios of how things could have been different. However, dwelling in guilt prevents us from moving forward. By forgiving ourselves and those who have wronged us, we break free from the cycle of blame and lamentation.

To illustrate, consider someone in a professional setting who blames themselves for a project's failure. This self-imposed guilt can lead to stress, anxiety, and decreased productivity. In contrast, if they accept their part in the situation, learn from it, and forgive themselves, they pave the way for future success. This change in mindset enables them to approach challenges with renewed energy and optimism, fostering a healthier work environment.

Furthermore, it's vital to recognize that accountability remains intact in the process of forgiveness. Forgiving someone doesn't mean that their actions are forgotten or that consequences disappear. Instead, it acknowledges that, while mistakes are made, individuals can still be held responsible. Accountability involves recognizing the impact of our actions and making amends where possible. Forgiveness, therefore, becomes an integral part of this journey, enabling growth while maintaining responsibility and justice.

This balance between forgiveness and accountability can be seen in various fields such as management, where leaders must address employee errors compassionately. A manager who forgives but also sets clear expectations demonstrates an understanding that people can improve when given a chance. By doing so, the team culture strengthens as individuals feel supported rather than judged, creating an atmosphere of trust and collaboration.

In cultivating a nonjudgmental mindset, we foster more love, peace, and gratitude. Letting go of judgments doesn't imply indifference or ignoring lessons learned. Rather, it opens us to understanding and appreciating diverse perspectives. Approaching situations without preconceived notions allows us to see potential opportunities rather than focusing solely on problems.

For example, in sales and marketing, embracing a nonjudgmental attitude helps professionals connect better with clients. When individuals are met with openness and genuine curiosity, they feel valued and understood. This approach builds stronger relationships based on mutual respect allowing for effective communication and long-term success. By practicing nonjudgment, we naturally cultivate gratitude for the connections we form and the experiences that shape our lives.

A practical guideline for surrounding ourselves with forgiveness involves being mindful of our thoughts and actions. Start by identifying areas where unforgiveness lingers—perhaps there's a colleague whose behavior irritates you or a personal disappointment that weighs heavily. Recognize these feelings without judgment and intentionally choose to forgive. Remember, forgiveness doesn't require forgetting; it's about altering your internal narrative and deciding not to let past events control your present and future actions.

Moreover, forgiveness serves as a demonstration that we are part of the peace and light of this world. By embodying forgiveness, we contribute positively to our surroundings, encouraging others to do the same. As individuals witness the benefits of a forgiving approach, they are inspired to adopt similar practices. This collective shift toward forgiveness creates ripple effects, benefiting communities and organizations alike.

Cultivating a Forgiving Mindset

In our lightning-paced, demanding world, forgiveness might seem like a distant concept—more of an abstract ideal than a practical approach to life. However, embracing forgiveness can lead us down the path to true fulfillment. At its core, forgiveness is not just about letting go of past grievances but also about freeing our minds from the shackles of negative emotions such as fear, sadness, and confusion.

Imagine your mind as a cluttered room. Each grudge or resentment you hold is like unwanted furniture that takes up space and blocks out the light. The unforgiving mind is often trapped in a cycle of fear and sadness, overwhelmed by the weight of unresolved conflicts. This internal turmoil breeds confusion, casting a shadow over even the clearest moments, obscuring our path to peace and personal growth. By holding on to past wrongs, we restrict ourselves from realizing our fullest potential, both personally and professionally.

Now, consider what happens when you start clearing the room. By embracing forgiveness, we open ourselves to clarity, strength, and enlightenment. It's akin to throwing open the windows and allowing fresh air to sweep through. With each act of forgiveness, we call upon the strength of our higher selves, inviting a profound sense of liberation and understanding. Suddenly, situations that once seemed tangled and murky become transparent, presenting opportunities for growth where there were only obstacles before.

The journey toward forgiveness and fulfillment isn't linear; it requires patience and faith in the timing of the universe. Trusting this timing helps support happiness in every circumstance we encounter. Rather than clinging to control, accepting that everything unfolds with purpose can bring great relief. This trust allows us to navigate life's ups and downs more harmoniously, knowing that every experience contributes to a larger tapestry. When we align with this flow, we find joy in unexpected places and embrace change as a friend rather than an adversary.

Surrounding oneself with forgiveness also has profound interpersonal benefits. Just as a positive outlook tends to attract more positivity, placing forgiveness at the center of our lives draws people who embody those same values—those who are forgiving, supportive, and compassionate. Who hasn't felt uplifted by the company of someone who forgives easily and harbors no grudges? These relationships provide safe spaces for vulnerability and authenticity, encouraging us to be our best selves without the fear of judgment or retaliation.

Consider the professional landscape. In fields like sales, marketing, and management, interactions with others form the backbone of success. An environment fostered by forgiveness can transform competitive tensions into collaborative triumphs. Colleagues who forgive create a culture of mutual respect and growth, reducing the stress of mistakes and misunderstandings while paving the way for innovative solutions. In turn, this mindset enhances productivity, fosters loyalty, and builds networks of support that extend beyond the workplace.

Athletes and entertainers, too, can benefit immensely from a forgiving perspective. Given the high-pressure stakes in these industries, learning to forgive oneself for failures or errors becomes crucial for maintaining mental balance and resilience. A forgiving mentality enables these professionals to bounce back stronger and wiser, turning setbacks into stepping stones for future achievements.

Forgiveness is a gift we give ourselves, a practice that offers abundant rewards. It encourages us to view challenges as opportunities for persistent striving and self-improvement. We must remember, however, that forgiveness doesn't mean condoning poor behavior or forgetting our experiences. Instead, it's about releasing the emotional grip these events have on us, allowing ourselves to heal and move forward with greater insight and peace.

Final Insights

Forgiveness isn't a onetime act—it's a daily practice. In this chapter, we explored how forgiveness, especially self-forgiveness, unlocks clarity, connection, and leadership. We reframed "sin" not as a moral sentence but as misalignment—moments when we lose sight of our highest self. And we saw that forgiveness isn't about excusing harm or forgetting what happened. It's about choosing alignment over ego. Growth over shame. Peace over punishment.

As professionals, leaders, and teammates, we carry far more than deadlines and metrics. We carry stories—of past mistakes, missed chances, and people we couldn't save. And yet, every day, we have a chance to choose a new story. One grounded in empathy, humility, and grace.

We saw this in Emma, a leader who couldn't forgive others until she learned to forgive herself. In the baseball player who found redemption not in stats but in service. And in the countless moments where leaders showed up with compassion, creating cultures of safety, resilience, and transformation.

Because when we forgive ourselves, we stop leading from defensiveness. And when we forgive others, we start leading from love.

Guidelines

- You can't give what you haven't given yourself. Clear the guilt, and you'll clear the path.
- When people feel seen—not judged—they grow. And when you listen for what's beneath the behavior, you'll build bridges others miss.
- After an interaction, ask: "Did that lift me up or drain me?" Surround yourself with people whose energy expands you.
- If someone deflects, gossips, or refuses accountability, protect your peace. Forgiveness doesn't require proximity.
- Forgiveness and boundaries are not opposites. Boundaries are how we love without losing ourselves.

Takeaways

- Forgiveness is freedom—from ego, resentment, and regret.
- Self-forgiveness is not indulgence—it's infrastructure.
- Empathy isn't soft. It's the sharpest tool in emotional leadership.
- You're not just curating your network—you're curating your nervous system.
- Forgiveness transforms conflict into connection—and shame into service.

Ask Yourself

- Am I holding on to something that no longer serves me?
- Am I giving myself and others the grace to grow?
- Am I creating a space where people feel safe to evolve?
- Where do I need to set a boundary that honors both empathy and self-respect?

The nature of forgiveness is fluid, not final. It's something we return to again and again, like breath. Like practice. And each time we choose it—each time we release the past and reclaim presence—we don't just change our relationships.

We change our reality.

Chapter 9

DICKSGIVING

Surround Yourself with Gratitude

We call it *Dicksgiving* not just because it's a time to show gratitude for the people we choose to do life and business with—but because it's a reminder that gratitude isn't seasonal. It's a strategy. It's the ultimate energetic frequency shift. And it's free.

Gratitude doesn't demand perfection. It demands practice. That's why we created the 30-Day Gratitude Challenge—not as a list of feel-good habits, but as a system for making thankfulness your default operating state. Can you go 30 days without acting like a dick? Without inviting or enabling dickish behavior into your life? That's the goal. Whether you're writing three things you're grateful for in a journal, saying "thank you" out loud before bed, or texting appreciation to someone who doesn't expect it, the goal is the same: to lower the bar for gratitude so far down that it becomes automatic.

Because here's the truth: The easiest things to do are also the easiest not to do. Saying thank you takes 0.1 seconds. It costs nothing.

But most people still won't do it. Not tonight. Not tomorrow morning. And certainly not three days from now. That's how fragile consistency is—and how critical it is to install gratitude, not just feel it.

This chapter explores how gratitude works not just as a mood booster, but as a mindset shift, a leadership tool, and a daily reset. It's not blind optimism. It's not about pretending everything's okay. It's about *acknowledgment*. About noticing what's right even when everything feels wrong.

Gratitude grounds us in what's true. It reminds us we're not alone. And when practiced with intention, it reorients our attention—away from fear, lack, and frustration—toward light, love, and lessons. It gives us a daily chance to see abundance over scarcity, beauty over chaos, connection over isolation.

Let's not just celebrate Dicksgiving once a year.

Let's live it—every day.

The Power of Gratitude

In life, it's easy to lose sight of the simple gestures that can transform both our personal well-being and professional interactions. I know I have time and time again, and time and time again have had wonderful people there to remind me. One such transformative gesture is gratitude. Expressing gratitude daily has a profound effect on our overall happiness and life satisfaction. Consider waking up each morning with a conscious effort to acknowledge at least one thing you're grateful for—be it your health, a supportive colleague, or simply the opportunity to start anew. This simple practice can change the entire trajectory of your day.

Imagine a sales professional who begins their day by jotting down three things they appreciate about their team. Over time, this habit not only elevates their mood but also encourages stronger team dynamics. When we express gratitude frequently, we train our brains to focus more on positives than negatives, leading to increased happiness and fulfillment in our lives. Research supports this, suggesting that regular expressions of gratitude can improve mental health and well-being significantly.

Beyond personal contentment, gratitude fosters a noncompetitive perspective that enhances personal fulfillment. In fields like marketing or entrepreneurship where competition can be fierce, adopting a mindset of gratitude helps shift focus from envy to appreciation. Instead of feeling threatened by a competitor's success, gratitude encourages professionals to celebrate their peers' achievements and recognize the unique strengths they bring to the table. This shift nurtures a healthier professional environment, where collaboration becomes more important than rivalry.

Take, for example, an advertising executive who acknowledges the creative ideas of others. When they express genuine admiration for a peer's successful campaign, they not only strengthen relationships but also reduce stress caused by unnecessary comparisons. By expressing gratitude, they open doors to new partnerships and opportunities that might have been overshadowed by competitive tension.

Similarly, practicing gratitude helps align thoughts and emotions with positivity and purpose. For many in management roles, where decisions impact teams and projects, remaining aligned with purpose ensures better outcomes. Gratitude allows managers to view setbacks as opportunities for growth rather than failures. Recognizing the dedication and hard work of their team during challenging times cultivates a motivated and resilient workforce ready to tackle future hurdles.

Consider a manager who regularly thanks their team for efforts both big and small. Acknowledging contributions improves morale and reinforces a sense of belonging and purpose. This approach influences how team members perceive their own roles and responsibilities, encouraging them to take ownership and strive for excellence.

Viewing challenges through a lens of gratitude shifts mental energy and outlook, turning obstacles into stepping stones. Within sports and entertainment, individuals face constant pressure and scrutiny. By viewing challenges with gratitude, athletes and performers can find renewed inspiration even in defeat, embracing loss as a lesson rather than a setback. Gratitude doesn't eliminate the difficulty of a challenge, but it transforms how these challenges are perceived.

For instance, an athlete grateful for their coach's critical feedback sees each piece of advice not as criticism, but as a path to perfection. They recognize the privilege of having mentors and resources at their disposal and channel this energy toward improvement. When faced with adversity, maintaining a gratitude mindset empowers them to overcome barriers, ultimately leading to a more enriching career.

Gratitude in Adversity

Amid life's challenges, gratitude emerges as a formidable ally, offering strength in moments of despair. Consider the remarkable journeys of stage-four cancer patients. Research has unveiled a compelling link between gratitude and higher survival rates among these individuals. The practice of gratitude seems to impart resilience, providing them with a renewed sense of purpose and determination. It's more than just a positive mindset; it's an acknowledgment of the small victories and the support received from loved ones, which together weave a safety net of hope.

This beacon of hope is not exclusive to those battling illness; it extends to anyone navigating through trauma or adversity. During traumatic experiences, maintaining a grateful attitude serves as an anchor, steadying one amid turbulent emotional currents. Gratitude nurtures resilience by shifting the focus from what is lost to what remains. It encourages individuals to appreciate their capacity to endure and adapt, fostering a mentality that seeks growth even in distress.

In relationships, gratitude acts as a bridge, mending rifts and enhancing satisfaction. Expressing gratitude within relationships does more than just strengthen bonds—it facilitates forgiveness, creating space for compassion and understanding. When people feel appreciated, tensions defuse, and conflicts are approached with empathy. In professional settings, too, acknowledging colleagues' efforts can lead to a more harmonious workplace environment, reducing stress and promoting collaboration.

Gratitude also encourages altruism and empathy, qualities that enrich social interactions. Grateful people are naturally inclined to be more empathetic, often going out of their way to assist others. This empathic drive stems from a keen awareness of the benefits they themselves have received—creating a cycle where gratitude begets generosity. For instance, in a corporate setting, a leader who regularly acknowledges the team's contributions may inspire team members to extend support to one another, fostering a culture of mutual aid and teamwork.

The transformative power of gratitude doesn't stop at personal improvement; its ripple effect influences broader communities. As individuals embrace gratitude, they tend to inspire those around them to adopt similar practices. This collective shift toward appreciation leads to a more engaged and supportive community, whether in families, workplaces, or neighborhoods.

Furthermore, the practice of gratitude enhances mental and emotional well-being, serving as a buffer against bitterness and negativity. By focusing on what we're thankful for, we diminish the impact of stressors and setbacks. Studies have shown that people who regularly practice gratitude report higher levels of optimism and lower levels of depression and anxiety.

For professionals operating in high-pressure environments, such as sales or entrepreneurship, cultivating gratitude can be particularly beneficial. It provides a much-needed counterbalance to competitiveness and performance pressure, encouraging a mindset that appreciates effort over outcome. In sports and entertainment, where public scrutiny can be intense, gratitude can ground individuals, helping them to maintain perspective and humility.

Consider the story of a sales manager who faced a challenging year with declining targets. Instead of succumbing to frustration, they chose to focus on gratitude—recognizing the team's hard work, the loyalty of longtime clients, and the lessons learned from failures. This shift in perspective not only alleviated stress but also motivated creative problem-solving, ultimately improving the team's performance.

Similarly, in entrepreneurial ventures, gratitude can fuel innovation and perseverance. Entrepreneurs often face uncertain paths and repeated setbacks. A grateful approach encourages them to learn from each experience, cherish the support network they have, and remain open to new opportunities.

However, it's important to note that gratitude isn't a cure-all. It's a tool, a mindset that requires consistent nurturing. Its true power unfolds when integrated into daily life, guiding reactions and influencing decisions during trying times.

Embracing gratitude involves a conscious choice to pause and reflect, to acknowledge the good even amid the bad. It invites us to see beyond immediate challenges, recognizing the growth potential they hold. By adopting this lens, we not only build inner strength but also foster environments rich in compassion, cooperation, and wisdom.

Building Gratitude Habits

To truly integrate gratitude into your daily life, embracing simple habits can make a significant difference. A cornerstone of an effective gratitude practice I've found is committing to saying "Thank you" twice daily. This might sound straightforward, but its impact is profound. By intentionally expressing gratitude, whether to a colleague who aided your project or a stranger holding the door open, you gradually cultivate a mindset focused on thankfulness.

This challenge encourages mindfulness, prompting you to actively seek moments in your day that deserve appreciation. With each "Thank you," you're not just acknowledging an act but fostering a culture of gratitude around you. The beauty lies in its simplicity; this practice requires minimal time yet delivers lasting benefits. You start noticing positive changes in your interactions as this habit becomes second nature, strengthening both personal and professional relationships.

Another powerful tool is regular journaling. Taking a few moments to jot down things you're grateful for heightens your awareness of life's abundance. It's like tuning your mind's antenna to pick up on positive frequencies. When you consistently catalog moments or people that bring joy, you begin to see patterns of blessings that may have previously gone unnoticed. This can be as simple as noting appreciation for a sunny day, a successful meeting, or a supportive friend.

A gratitude journal doesn't need to be elaborate. Keep it accessible—a small notebook by your bedside or a notes app on your phone works perfectly. The key is consistency. Over time, you'll find yourself naturally looking for things to write about, training your mind to spot gratitude-worthy moments throughout the day. This practice not only enhances your mood but also builds resilience, helping you focus on the positives even amid challenges.

Developing gratitude is akin to muscle memory. Just as athletes tirelessly repeat drills to prepare for competition, practicing gratitude makes it automatic. At first, you might need reminders to pause and give thanks, but with repetition, it becomes effortless. You begin to appreciate everyday occurrences without conscious effort, much like how habitual runners find themselves itching for a jog. This transformation is gradual, yet impactful, embedding gratitude deep within your psyche.

Incorporating gratitude exercises into your routine is much like exercising any other skill—it requires dedication and patience. Start small, perhaps with just one minute of reflection per day, then gradually expand as it feels natural. Imagine each moment of gratitude as a tiny seed planted in your mind. With care, it blooms, enriching your perspective, making gratitude not just an activity but a lifestyle.

Teaching children gratitude early sets them on a path toward lifelong happiness and empathy. Children often mirror adult behaviors, so modeling gratitude can have a lasting impact. Encourage kids to share three things they are thankful for at dinner or before bed. This simple practice helps them recognize and express appreciation, developing emotional intelligence from a young age.

Children are inherently curious, and integrating gratitude into their daily routine shapes their worldview positively. They learn to value not just material gifts but experiences and relationships. Instilling these habits early fosters an attitude of generosity and kindness, preparing them to navigate life's ups and downs with a balanced outlook.

Evaluating Through Gratitude

I've had plenty of days where slowing down to think about gratitude felt like a luxury I didn't have time for. But I've always been rewarded when I slowed down and made the time. Though it can feel like one more to-do, embracing gratitude can provide profound insights into evaluating personal and professional scenarios. One effective way to achieve this is through the practice of mental subtraction, which involves imagining the absence of something valued in your life. This exercise isn't about fostering negative thoughts but rather about highlighting what truly matters. Visualize the lack of a supportive team or the guiding mentor you've had throughout your career. Such reflections can deepen appreciation for seemingly small yet significant aspects of your work environment.

Consider the story of Alex, a marketing manager who was overwhelmed by projects. By engaging in mental subtraction during a quiet moment each morning, Alex started appreciating her dedicated team more sincerely. She realized that without their support, her achievements wouldn't be possible.

This realization not only increased her own job satisfaction but also encouraged her to express gratitude more openly, fostering a stronger sense of teamwork and accomplishment within her department.

To further build on gratitude, keeping a gratitude journal can be a transformative practice. In the hustle of our daily lives, it's easy to overlook the positives. Writing down things you're grateful for shifts focus from the pressures of deadlines and targets to the rewards embedded in your journey. This habit also sharpens our ability to recognize opportunities and successes in our professional spheres that may otherwise go unnoticed.

Imagine Jonathan, an entrepreneur grappling with startup challenges. By maintaining a gratitude journal, he identified little victories—a positive client review, a successful pitch, or even an invigorating coffee break with his team. These entries served as reminders during tough times, reinforcing a more constructive mindset. Over time, he found himself less stressed, armed with a stronger belief in his capabilities and a greater enthusiasm for tackling obstacles.

Gratitude has the power to improve performance and satisfaction within the workplace. When we consciously appreciate our colleagues' contributions, it often leads to environments rife with encouragement and cooperation. In cultures where gratitude is genuinely practiced, feedback is not just a formality but a meaningful exchange that bolsters morale and motivation.

One of the most powerful gratitude practices I've discovered doesn't happen during meditation or journaling. It happens during hiring.

Let me explain.

Every so often, I post job listings for positions that are already filled. Not because I'm looking to replace anyone. Not because I'm trying to stir the pot. But because it gives me a deeper understanding and appreciation for what I already have.

When I go through the process of reviewing résumés, conducting interviews, and comparing skill sets, something beautiful happens. I gain perspective. I start to see just how special my current team really is. I notice the irreplaceable traits—the empathy, the loyalty, the emotional intelligence—that don't show up on a résumé. I start finding the light, the love, and the lessons in the people I've already chosen to build with.

It also shows me what is replicable and what is rare. Which skills we can develop in-house and which ones we need to go find. It becomes a strategic mirror, a way to measure our strengths, our gaps, and our future scalability.

And here's the best part. By staying in touch with the talent that is out there, I'm never caught off guard. I'm always planting seeds. Always building relationships. So, when it is time to grow, I'm not starting from scratch. I'm simply aligning the right people to the right positions at the right time.

So my advice is this. Always interview for roles you have already filled.

Not out of fear. Out of gratitude. Out of vision. Out of a desire to elevate what you have while preparing for what is coming.

Because when you truly know the value of who is beside you, you'll start seeing every person on your team not just as an employee but as a blessing and a bridge to something even greater.

By focusing on gratitude, one maintains a constructive view despite challenges. This isn't about ignoring failures or difficulties but rather approaching them with a mindset that seeks solutions and growth opportunities. Facing adversity with an underlying layer of gratitude allows for resilience to shine through, turning potential setbacks into stepping stones.

For instance, take Sam, a sports agent who often faced last-minute deal negotiations and competitive challenges. By adopting a gratitude-centered perspective, he learned to value lessons from lost deals and celebrated every small breakthrough. Instead of dwelling on disappointments, Sam now approaches each challenge with a balanced outlook, ensuring gratitude remains at the heart of his professional journey.

For professionals across varied fields, nurturing this mindset can transform not only individual experiences but also entire organizational cultures. Encourage yourself and others to see gratitude not merely as a fleeting emotion but as a rewarding practice that enhances both personal fulfillment and professional success.

Empowering Others Through Gratitude

Gratitude is a powerful tool that doesn't just elevate the individual but also radiates positivity, enhancing connections amongst people. When we make an effort to incorporate gratitude into our daily interactions, it opens up a space for stronger and more meaningful family relationships. Imagine a family dinner where each member shares something they're thankful for; it not only deepens bonds but creates an atmosphere of warmth and mutual respect. Acknowledging small gestures, like thanking a family member for helping with chores or simply being there during tough times, can shift the dynamic from one of taking things for granted to one of appreciation and understanding.

Moreover, when adults model gratitude, especially in family settings, it sets a powerful example for children. Young minds are incredibly impressionable and observing their parents or guardians demonstrate gratitude helps instill these values early on. Children who see gratitude in action often learn empathy and kindness as they grow. They begin to understand the importance of valuing other people's contributions, which is a lesson that stays with them throughout life. This nurturing environment fosters emotionally intelligent individuals who appreciate the little things and acknowledge the support they receive.

The impact of gratitude extends beyond family life into community and organizational cultures. It's like a domino effect where one expression of gratitude can lead to another, creating a ripple of positivity. In workplaces, acknowledging a colleague's hard work and successes can boost morale and foster teamwork. This positive reinforcement encourages a supportive atmosphere and strengthens professional relationships, making the workplace a more enjoyable and productive environment. The same holds true within communities; gratitude-based initiatives, such as community service projects or simple recognition of efforts, can enhance communal relations and cooperation.

Furthermore, gratitude offers remarkable benefits in the face of personal setbacks. Accelerating appreciation—the process of quickly identifying and focusing on aspects of life for which one is grateful—can act as a rapid mood enhancer during challenging times. For instance, after a difficult day at work, instead of dwelling on what went wrong, shifting focus to what worked well or what lessons can be learned has the potential to uplift spirits and restore optimism. This mental shift nurtures resilience and aids in overcoming adversities by focusing on positives rather than spiraling into negative thought patterns.

Incorporating gratitude into daily routines doesn't have to be complex or time-consuming. Simple acts such as starting meetings with expressions of thanks or ending the day by jotting down three things you're grateful for can profoundly affect emotional health and interpersonal dynamics. These practices promote a mindset of abundance, turning mundane moments into opportunities for joy and connection.

Recognizing the broader impact of gratitude invites us to actively cultivate it in various areas of our lives. By doing so, we not only enrich our own experiences but also contribute positively to the environments around us. Whether it's through strengthening family ties, educating children, enhancing workplace culture, or building resilient attitudes, gratitude is a catalyst for transformative change. Its power lies in its simplicity, yet it has the capacity to profoundly influence how we relate to ourselves and to others.

Final Insights

Gratitude isn't just a feeling—it's a frequency. A practice. A choice. And in fast-paced, high-pressure environments, it's one of the simplest, most powerful tools we have to shift not just our mindset, but our relationships, performance, and peace of mind.

Throughout this chapter, we explored how gratitude works like a magnet. It pulls in the right energy, the right people, the right perspective. When you live in gratitude, you don't just feel better—you make others feel better too. You become magnetic. People want to be around someone who sees the light in every room, even when it's dim. That's leadership. That's legacy.

Gratitude also builds resilience. Whether you're facing setbacks in your business, burnout in your body, or friction in your team, gratitude grounds you in what's still good. It shifts your attention from lack to abundance, from judgment to appreciation, from isolation to empathy.

And here's the key: It only works if you work it. Gratitude doesn't require perfection. It requires practice. When you embed gratitude into your daily rhythm—when you train your mind to look for what's working—you transform the way you show up, not just for others, but for yourself.

Guidelines

- Say thank you when you wake up. Say thank you before bed. Anchor the day in appreciation.
- After every interaction, check: Did this person lift me up or wear me down? Don't ignore the answer.
- Negativity spreads. So does grace. Choose the energy you want to be contagious.
- Saying no doesn't make you a jerk. It makes you intentional. Boundaries aren't rejection—they're respect.
- Gratitude isn't just about being thankful—it's about being **aware**. Of others. Of effort. Of the energy you bring into the room.

Takeaways

- Gratitude is a leadership tool, not a luxury.
- What you focus on expands—so focus on what's working.
- Your energy is contagious. Be the person who lifts the room.
- Empathy grows from gratitude. They're teammates, not opposites.
- A grateful life isn't a perfect life—it's a practiced one.

Ask Yourself

- Who in my life makes me feel more like me when I'm around them?
- When was the last time I showed real appreciation to someone in my circle?
- What energy am I projecting? Do people feel uplifted or drained after they leave my presence?

Let's stop treating gratitude like a once-a-year concept that we channel during a once-a-year holiday. Let's live it like a habit. Because when you practice gratitude, you don't just change your day. You change your direction. You change your vibration. And that changes everything.

Chapter 10

LOW BLOWS

Surround Yourself with Accountability

Accountability is one of the most misunderstood concepts in modern life—and one of the most transformative. People often confuse it with liability, but they're not the same. Liability is legal. Accountability is personal. It doesn't live in courtrooms—it lives in the mirror.

A few years ago, I was stopped at a red light, minding my own business, when—*bam*—a car slammed into me from behind. The driver had been texting, not paying attention. Legally, it was straightforward: He was liable. His insurance covered the damage, and I did everything I was supposed to do—filed a claim, spoke with my attorney, got the car repaired.

But that was just one layer of the experience.

Here's where accountability came in. Instead of stopping at blame, I asked myself a different set of questions. Ones most people never even consider:

- What did I do to attract this situation into my life?
- What am I supposed to learn from it?
- How am I participating in the perception of this event, and what lesson is embedded in that perception?

See, accountability doesn't mean ignoring reality. It means elevating your awareness. It means shifting from "Why me?" to "What for?"

And what I realized was powerful. That day, I had been rushing. Emotionally scattered. Energetically misaligned. Even though I was doing everything "right," I was vibrating at a frequency of chaos—and the universe delivered me a perfectly inconvenient little lesson to match.

That accident wasn't punishment. It was protection. It wasn't bad luck. It was a promotion. It wasn't chaos. It was a wake-up call, disguised as a low-speed collision.

That's the difference: Liability settles a score. Accountability raises your vibration. It's the unseen force that holds everything together. It's what keeps leaders grounded, teams aligned, and personal growth on track. It asks us to take radical responsibility for not just what we do, but how we show up. It invites us to own our energy, our patterns, and the ripple effects of our actions.

This chapter explores how accountability becomes a superpower when practiced with intention. Whether you're leading a company, building a brand, or simply navigating a difficult season, the question is the same: Are you willing to own your part—not just when things go wrong, but when things go quiet?

Because the truth is, accountability doesn't end with an apology or a checklist. It begins with presence. It's the daily decision to ask,

"How am I contributing to this outcome?"—and then do something about it.

Understanding Accountability

Personal accountability means taking ownership not just for the triumphs but also for the stumbles along our journey. Many people are quick to claim credit when things go well but become experts at pointing fingers when challenges arise. True accountability demands that we assess our roles in every situation, acknowledging both our strengths and faults. This process requires a level of humility and introspection that can be challenging yet rewarding.

Taking responsibility isn't limited to owning up to mistakes or lapses in judgment. It's a continuous commitment, a lens through which we view our contribution to the outcomes that shape our lives. Suppose an advertising campaign doesn't hit its targets. Instead of blaming the team for lacking creativity or the market conditions for being unfavorable, it's essential to reflect on your contributions. Were there signs you overlooked? Did you push hard enough for innovative ideas? When we do this, we learn valuable lessons and pave the way for future successes based on informed decisions rather than assumptions.

Falling into the trap of blaming others or justifying poor outcomes might seem appealing initially. These actions can serve as temporary Band-Aids—quick fixes that allow us to sidestep uncomfortable truths. But, over time, relying on blame can erode our personal integrity and strain professional relationships. For instance, if a project fails due to miscommunication, shifting the blame onto colleagues might protect your ego, but it could damage team cohesion. Resentment builds, trust diminishes, and collaboration suffers.

This negative cycle not only influences workplace dynamics but also spills over into personal life. Relationships that thrive on honesty and mutual respect can falter if one party consistently deflects responsibility. Imagine how trust would crumble if every interaction turned into a game of defense, with each person shielding their vulnerabilities instead of addressing the core issues. The heart of accountability lies in recognizing the opportunity for growth and improvement with each misstep and lapse.

One of the most powerful results of embracing accountability is the cultivation of truthfulness. By admitting faults and errors with sincerity, we embrace authenticity. This honesty fosters personal growth, accelerating our development beyond what we thought possible. Truthfulness becomes a cornerstone of our character, something people can rely on both personally and professionally.

Incorporating this mindset takes intentionality and practice. Begin by reflecting on past experiences—both successful ventures and those that could have gone better. Analyze your contributions objectively and without judgment. As you identify patterns and areas for growth, strategize ways to alter your behavior moving forward. Consistently applying these reflections helps build a habit of accountability that becomes second nature over time.

As professionals, we are often tasked with making decisions that impact others—from our immediate teams to larger organizational structures. When we nurture accountability, others will notice. They'll see someone who stands firm in their truth, admits when they fall short, and consistently aims to improve. This reliability builds trust and can inspire others to adopt a similar approach.

After all, leading by example is one of the most effective teaching tools available.

Moreover, accountability has a ripple effect. Beyond boosting personal integrity, it enhances the culture within workplaces. Teams that prioritize accountability operate with a clear understanding of shared goals and individual responsibilities. This clarity reduces confusion and enables focused energy on solutions rather than assigning blame.

Leaders play a pivotal role in championing this change. By embodying accountability, they set a high standard for their teams, showcasing the importance of personal responsibility. Rather than fostering environments where blame prevails, leaders can encourage open dialogue and learning from mistakes. When missteps occur, focus discussions on collective improvements rather than individual shortcomings.

Yet, it's crucial to recognize that accountability doesn't imply perfection. There will always be room for error in complex situations. Instead, accountability means striving for excellence while accepting the inherent imperfections that come with human endeavors. The key is maintaining an open mind toward feedback and growth, turning setbacks into stepping stones.

Encouraging an environment where accountability is valued does wonders for organizations aiming for long-term success. Employees feel empowered to take ownership of tasks, knowing that their contributions matter and their developments are acknowledged. It cultivates loyalty and productivity—an engaged workforce ready to push boundaries and tackle challenges with determination.

For those venturing into entrepreneurship or seeking to climb the corporate ladder, mastering accountability becomes a strategic advantage. Clients, partners, and stakeholders gravitate toward trustworthy individuals willing to own their actions, creating authentic connections grounded in mutual respect.

To instill the principles of accountability, consider adopting small actionable steps into daily routines. Set aside time for self-reflection, evaluate choices made throughout the day, and consider alternative approaches. Encourage feedback from peers and superiors—another avenue for learning and refining accountability skills.

By promoting accountability across all facets of life, whether handling personal finances or managing large-scale projects, its positive influence extends far beyond immediate results. It becomes an enduring habit that shapes our character, interactions, and overall quality of life.

Consequences of Lying

In the complex tapestry of human interaction, lies weave a particularly damaging thread. As we delve into how deceit affects relationships and trust, we must acknowledge that lying is more than just an isolated act of dishonesty; it is a behavior that profoundly disconnects individuals. In working environments, where collaboration is often key to success, honesty serves as the foundation upon which professional relationships should be built. When someone resorts to lying, either to avoid conflict or to gain a perceived advantage, it creates a rift, sowing seeds of doubt that can spread like wildfire.

Consider a scenario on a quick-acting sales team. Trust is critical, with each member relying on others to provide accurate data and insights. If one person intentionally provides misleading information, it might initially seem to accomplish their goals, perhaps securing a deal or impressing a manager. However, once this deception comes to light, the repercussions are far-reaching. It not only damages the individual's credibility but also disrupts the team's harmony, creating an atmosphere of suspicion and uncertainty. The initial disconnection stretches further, affecting not just the people directly involved but the team's overall morale and efficiency.

The ultimate betrayal isn't merely the lie itself; rather, it's the continuous effort to cover it up. This entanglement in deception erodes relationships more deeply. Imagine an advertising executive who misrepresents campaign results to upper management. Initially, they may feel they've dodged a bullet. But maintaining this facade requires increasingly elaborate deception, spiraling into a web of lies that becomes harder to manage. Each layer of concealment represents another tear in the fabric of trust, slowly unraveling the relationship between the executive and their colleagues. Once colleagues begin to question the integrity of the executive, the damage can prove irreparable.

Human nature often propels us toward truth, even when we momentarily stray from it. There exists a natural yearning for stability and reliability in our interactions, especially in professional settings where teamwork and collaboration are vital. This need underscores the importance of trust as the cornerstone of any meaningful relationship.

Without trust, interpersonal connections falter, leaving behind partnerships riddled with anxiety and apprehension. In industries like marketing or media, where personal rapport and networking are pivotal, the absence of trust can lead to isolation and a breakdown of essential communication channels.

Consider athletes in the sports industry, where teamwork and trust are not just beneficial but essential to performance. A team thrives on the belief that every member will put forth their best effort, transparently sharing strengths, weaknesses, and any challenges faced. If an athlete consistently embellishes their fitness level or underreports injuries, what initially seems like self-preservation quickly devolves into team-wide mistrust. Not only does this erode confidence in the individual, but it also compromises team dynamics, potentially leading to losses both on and off the field.

In contrast, honesty nurtures trust, paving the way for sincere and effective communication. When individuals are transparent about their intentions, goals, and mistakes, they build solid foundations for growth and collaboration. In workplaces fraught with deadlines and high stakes, such transparency fosters an environment where team members feel valued and respected. Marketing agencies, for example, depend on innovative ideas flowing freely and without fear of judgment. A culture rooted in honesty encourages creativity, fostering a productive environment where clients and team members alike thrive on mutual respect.

This critical connection between honesty and trust highlights why accountability cannot be overstated. Leaders within organizations are tasked with setting standards for behavior. They must embody values that reflect a commitment to transparency, ensuring these principles ripple throughout their teams. By cultivating a culture of accountability, leaders not only reinforce honesty but actively dismantle environments where deceit could take root. This proactive stance builds resilient teams fortified by trust, capable of weathering market fluctuations and competitive pressures with unified strength.

Guidelines play a crucial role here, particularly in work environments. Establishing clear policies around honesty and integrity enables employees to understand expectations and align their actions accordingly. Encouraging open discussions about mistakes and learning opportunities fosters a culture where team members support each other, viewing errors as stepping stones rather than stumbling blocks. Such frameworks are indispensable in preventing the insidious spread of distrust, safeguarding both individual careers and organizational health.

Ultimately, nurturing a climate of honesty transcends mere professional etiquette—it reshapes entire organizational cultures. When truth underpins every interaction, both internally and externally, businesses forge strong alliances with stakeholders, customers, and employees alike. The insurance provided by consistent truthfulness is invaluable, offering security in knowing that all parties involved uphold shared values of integrity and respect.

Thus, the path to genuine and resilient relationships—whether in sales, entrepreneurship, or media—is paved with honesty. Lies may appear tempting in the short term, offering quick fixes or easy paths to success. Yet, they inherently undermine the very structures our interactions rely on. By embracing transparency and maintaining trust, we ensure that our personal and professional relationships are not only intact but flourish in an ever-evolving world. As we conclude our exploration of how lies affect relationships and trust, it is imperative to remember that the integrity of our words defines the strength of our bonds, steering us toward a future rich with possibility and grounded in unshakable confidence.

Accountability Versus Liability

Understanding the distinction between accountability and liability can significantly impact both personal and professional growth. At first glance, these terms might appear synonymous, yet they hold different implications and applications in our lives. Accountability transcends mere legal obligations, delving into a more profound realm where personal and professional development takes center stage.

Accountability is about owning our actions and recognizing their influence. Consider a marketing manager whose campaign fails to meet set targets. Instead of focusing solely on external factors, such as market trends or consumer behavior, an accountable individual reflects on their strategic choices. Did the campaign align with consumer preferences? Was the message clear and engaging? This introspective approach helps them learn from experience, avoiding the pitfalls of blame-shifting.

In contrast, liability frequently relates to legal responsibility—a concept embedded in contracts and regulations. For instance, a company might find itself liable if a product defect causes harm, necessitating compensation to affected parties. Here, the emphasis lies on financial or legal repercussions rather than personal growth. Hence, distinguishing between these two constructs fosters a deeper understanding of how individuals can navigate their roles effectively.

Accountability invites personal reflection, promoting learning opportunities and growth. It encourages professionals to assess their contributions honestly, paving the way for constructive change. Imagine an advertising executive who notices decreasing viewership for broadcasted ads. They could easily attribute this to external digital competition, but an accountable mindset prompts self-evaluation. Is there innovation in their content? Are they reaching the right audience? This evaluative process not only identifies weaknesses but also unveils potential areas for improvement, leading to career advancement.

Moreover, embracing accountability nurtures a mindset conducive to forgiveness and acceptance of life's lessons. We often encounter setbacks and challenges in our journeys, whether due to our own mistakes or unforeseeable circumstances. By acknowledging our role and influence, we develop resilience and adaptability. Take, for instance, a sports team that loses a crucial match. The players can choose to blame poor refereeing or bad weather, yet true growth springs from examining their performance: Were tactics applied effectively? Did teamwork falter under pressure? Through this lens, they cultivate maturity, empowering themselves to overcome future hurdles.

Including guidelines for differentiating between accountability and liability can solidify this understanding further. Accountability emphasizes personal influence over outcomes, encouraging a broader perspective on cause and effect. Unlike liability focused on legal consequences, accountability is inherently proactive. To illustrate, entrepreneurs launching a new business venture face myriad uncertainties. While securing trademarks and patents addresses liability concerns, accountability involves continuous market research and evaluation of consumer needs to enhance service delivery.

Professionals can benefit from adopting specific strategies to foster accountability. Firstly, cultivate an environment where feedback is valued, rendering learning a communal experience. Secondly, set realistic and measurable goals, allowing for objective self-assessment. Lastly, practice humility by admitting mistakes and seeking ways to improve. These practices ensure that accountability becomes a habitual aspect of our personal and professional ethos, driving consistent progress and fulfillment.

Accountability in Relationships

Accountability is more than just taking ownership. It's our ability to learn—from how we behave, who we attract, and how we choose to interpret what's happening around us.

When I was younger, I didn't fully understand that. I surrounded myself with the wrong people and bought into the wrong ideas. I thought I was just having fun, networking, being part of the crowd. But looking back, those choices shaped the energy I brought into my marriage, my friendships, and my business.

One example still weighs on me. I had a close friend who consistently cheated on his wife. He told us they had an open marriage, that everything was fine. But we knew it wasn't. We'd see him show up to football games with a different woman almost every time, and we'd all pretend it was normal—even though his wife was our friend too.

Now, to be clear, I never lied for him. I didn't cover his tracks. I even told him I disagreed with what he was doing. But I also didn't speak up. I stayed silent. And that silence had consequences.

Years later, my wife and I still carry scars from the environment we allowed ourselves to live in—surrounded by people who didn't honor their commitments. Even though neither of us stepped outside our marriage, we both lived with a lingering fear. What if they did? What if I did?

That's the invisible tax of participating in the perception of something you know is wrong.

See, accountability isn't just about whether you were the one cheating or lying. It's about whether you were learning. Whether you held the standard. Whether you said something.

I wasn't part of the lie directly. But I was responsible for not speaking truth. I attracted more people like that into my life because I didn't draw a line. I stayed silent, I showed up, I pretended things were fine—and that's what accountability really is.

It's asking, "What am I supposed to learn from this?"

It's asking, "What role did I play in allowing this energy into my life?"

It's not punishment. It's perspective.

It's the power to turn guilt into growth. Regret into responsibility.

Because when we own our part fully, we begin to raise the vibration of who we are and who we allow into our lives. And we stop paying for the lies of the past by finally living in truth.

In today's interconnected world, accountability is the bedrock of healthy relationships—both personal and professional. At the core of any strong bond is honest communication, which helps prevent misunderstandings and builds durable trust. Whether you're working with colleagues or deepening relationships at home, transparency strengthens the foundation.

Take a marketing team racing toward a campaign launch. When everyone is clear on their role and able to speak up honestly when something goes wrong, problems get solved quickly and trust grows stronger. The same applies in your personal life. Clear communication about expectations and emotions avoids confusion and conflict. Every honest exchange becomes a brick in the bridge of mutual respect.

In contrast, lies breed insecurity. Even minor untruths erode connection and can create a gap that widens over time. Think of a manager who tweaks a sales report to look better. That moment of dishonesty may seem small—but when discovered, it wrecks credibility and trust with the team. In relationships, repeated dishonesty builds emotional walls and distances people who once felt close.

Truth, on the other hand, is what fosters security and intimacy.

It gives us the safety to show up fully—without fear, without posturing. When we prioritize honesty, we create the conditions for others to do the same. And when that happens, relationships deepen.

Truthfulness also signals leadership. A founder who's transparent with their clients earns loyalty. A friend who consistently tells the truth, even when it's hard, becomes someone others rely on. Truth builds reputation; reputation builds opportunity.

But that kind of leadership starts with internal alignment. It starts with being honest with yourself about the energy you carry, the people you tolerate, and the stories you're still telling. That's the work of accountability. And here's the most powerful truth of all: When you raise your own standards for truth, you start attracting people who live by the same.

Accountability and Personal Freedom

Never forget that accountability isn't just a buzzword; it's a key to unlocking personal freedom and fulfillment. It might seem paradoxical at first: How does accepting responsibility for our actions lead to freedom? The answer lies in the power that comes with owning our decisions and their consequences.

Imagine you're an entrepreneur launching a new product. The market response is lukewarm, and you're faced with numerous challenges. Here's where accountability becomes your ally. By taking ownership of both success and failure, you gain control over your future decisions. Instead of viewing setbacks as failures, they become learning opportunities—paving the way for innovation and growth. True freedom emanates from understanding that, while we can't control every outcome, we can decide how to respond to them.

Resilience thrives in environments where challenges are seen as instructional rather than punitive. Consider an athlete who misses out on a long-desired victory. Rather than dwelling on defeat, accountability encourages this athlete to analyze their performance objectively. What went wrong? How can it be improved next time? This mindset shift from self-criticism to self-improvement instills resilience, equipping professionals across various fields—from sales to sports—with the optimism needed to persevere through adversity.

Accountability reshapes narratives. Think about a marketing manager who faces criticism after an unsuccessful campaign. Instead of making excuses, the manager owns up to the missteps and scrutinizes the strategy with fresh eyes. This proactive approach transforms a potential story of failure into one of redemption and triumph—an inspiring tale that not only uplifts the individual but also motivates the entire team to rise and innovate.

In professional settings, truthfulness is integral to crafting stories that inspire rather than deter. When individuals live truthfully, accountability naturally follows. An agent in the entertainment industry, for instance, who transparently communicates with their clients fosters trust and creativity. By replacing excuses with honest dialogues, they lay the foundation for lasting professional relationships based on mutual respect and shared goals.

It is crucial to understand how honesty impacts energy and trust within teams and organizations. A guideline here would emphasize the importance of transparency. Consistent truthfulness enhances collaboration by building a culture of trust where ideas flow freely. When employees know their opinions are valued and their contributions recognized, they're more engaged and motivated, further driving organizational success.

Similarly, storytelling can serve as either an excuse or inspiration.

A vital guideline is to always aim for the latter. Transform excuses into empowering stories by acknowledging past mistakes and highlighting the lessons learned. This approach not only elevates personal morale but also resonates with colleagues who see vulnerability as strength and encouragement to embrace their unique journeys.

Finally, connecting to goodness through accountability enriches both personal and professional experiences. Accountability invites introspection, urging individuals to align their actions with their core values. Whether in management, media, or journalism, professionals who practice accountability navigate their careers with integrity and purpose. They actively contribute to a positive work environment where ethics and excellence thrive hand in hand.

Final Insights

Accountability isn't about blame—it's about awareness. When we choose to see every situation, even the uncomfortable ones, as invitations to learn, we stop being victims of our circumstances and start becoming architects of our lives. This chapter explored the difference between liability and true accountability—not what's legal or expected, but what's aligned and expansive.

We saw how accountability operates not only in our individual choices, but in our relationships: what we allow, what we attract, and what we stay silent about. It's about the energy we carry, the boundaries we set, and the truth we choose to speak (or don't). Owning our part—especially when it's subtle or unspoken—is how we begin to shift what shows up in our lives.

Whether it's a fender bender, a broken friendship, or a workplace tension, asking "What role did I play?" turns guilt into growth and regret into responsibility. That's not weakness. That's power. When we hold ourselves to that standard, we elevate everyone around us.

Guidelines

- Low moments can be high mirrors. Let them teach you something.
- Silence is still participation.
- Ask yourself what (or who) you're attracting—and why.
- One helps you grow; the other keeps you stuck.

Takeaways

- Accountability isn't about guilt—it's about alignment.
- You're responsible not just for your actions, but for what you tolerate.
- True accountability builds trust—in yourself and from others.
- Owning your role creates freedom from old stories and stuck patterns.
- You attract what you allow. Raise your standard, and your circle will shift.

Ask Yourself

- Where in my life am I staying silent when I need to speak?
- What relationships or patterns keep repeating—and what am I meant to learn from them?
- Am I showing up in alignment with the values I expect from others?
- Who do I become when no one's watching—and is that person someone I trust?

And maybe it all comes back to that moment at the red light. Maybe you've had one just like I did all those years ago.

On paper, it wasn't your fault. But accountability isn't about paperwork—it's about perception. It's about asking, *What energy was I carrying? What lesson was I being offered?*

That's the shift. When you start looking at every "accident" as an assignment, every disruption as a direction, you stop seeing life as something that happens to you—and start realizing it's happening for you, through you. That's the real power of accountability. It turns a fender bender into a frequency reset. A low blow into a higher standard. And it puts your hands back on the wheel.

Chapter 11

A DICK IS A DICK

Surround Yourself with Effective Communication

A dick is a dick, no matter where you find them—in the office, on the road, or even within yourself. Encountering difficult personalities is an inevitable part of life, and navigating these interactions effectively becomes crucial, not just for personal sanity but also for professional success. While we often wish to avoid these encounters, they provide unique opportunities to hone our communication skills and grow within our respective fields. Understanding the dynamics at play when dealing with such characters can transform these challenges into pivotal learning experiences that enrich our professional journeys.

When it comes to growth, especially through communication, there are three zones we cycle through.

First is the *comfort zone*. It's where things are easy. Familiar. Safe. But here's the truth: Nothing grows there. In fact, the longer you stay in that zone, the smaller it gets. Stay too long and it starts to constrict, like a house that shrinks over time, until eventually you're trapped in a room so small you can't even get out of bed. I've seen people get stuck there. I've been there.

Just outside that is the *learning zone*. This is where expansion happens. It's where you feel stretched but not broken. Challenged but not overwhelmed. It's where your capabilities grow, your confidence compounds, and your communication begins to connect in new ways—deeper, more authentic, more impactful.

But then, just beyond that, there's the *anxiety zone*. That's where the fear lives. Where our insecurities get loud. It's where we're out of alignment, pushing too hard, too fast, and too far beyond our capacity. Spend too much time in the anxiety zone and it doesn't just stop your growth; it reverses it. That zone shrinks the same way the comfort zone does. And when it collapses on you, you can find yourself physically, emotionally, even spiritually unable to move forward.

I learned this lesson the hard way.

When I left for college, I spent three days smack in the middle of what felt like Smogville, California. I was completely outside my comfort zone. Everything was unfamiliar. The air was thick, the environment intense, and I was trying to push through it, thinking I could just grind my way into growth.

But here's what I didn't realize at the time. I had passed the learning zone and went straight into anxiety. I ignored the signals. I kept pushing. And eventually, my body pushed back. I started coughing up blood. I couldn't make practice. I couldn't focus. My system shut down.

That moment taught me something priceless. Effective communication isn't about how far you can stretch. It's about knowing how far to stretch without snapping. Growth happens on the edge but not off the cliff.

So now, I lead with intention. I communicate with awareness. I test the edge of my learning zone every day, but I don't live in the anxiety zone. I've learned to calibrate where I am, stretch just enough, and trust that consistent growth always outperforms occasional burnout.

That's how we grow stronger. That's how we communicate better. And most importantly, that's how we stay aligned with ourselves and with others.

In this chapter, we delve into the art of surrounding yourself with effective communication, equipping you with strategies to handle difficult personalities with grace and poise. By exploring various techniques, readers will gain insights into how effective communication can mitigate tension and foster productive relationships. Maintaining a balance between assertiveness and empathy is also crucial in enhancing our ability to navigate the complex interactions. Through relatable narratives and practical advice, you will discover how adopting a positive communication style can create an atmosphere conducive to collaboration and mutual respect in any professional setting.

The Importance of Content in Communication

At its core, content acts as the heartbeat of any communication strategy, serving as the vehicle through which ideas are shared and connections are formed. In scenarios ranging from a sales pitch to a media campaign, the substance of what you convey shapes perceptions and drives engagement. Content isn't just about information; it's about delivering that information effectively to resonate with an audience.

The longevity of good content contributes significantly to its power. Timeless content endures because it offers value beyond immediate comprehension, influencing thought and behavior not only today but also tomorrow. This capability of enduring influence is particularly crucial in sectors like advertising and entertainment, where the ability to captivate audiences over time determines success. When content remains relevant, it continuously attracts positive engagement, expanding its reach and solidifying its influence over time.

Consider Mickey Mouse, a prime example of content with lasting impact. Created nearly a century ago, Mickey has transcended generations and maintained his appeal across various platforms and cultures. The character's ongoing popularity highlights how powerful content can thrive long after its creation. It embodies principles that resonate universally, ensuring Mickey remains a beloved symbol within both households and industries alike. His presence expands far beyond animation, affecting merchandise, theme parks, and even broader media narratives.

Content must vibrate at a higher rate according to our book's philosophy if it is to achieve a lasting impact. This concept goes beyond conventional understanding, suggesting that ideas need energy and vitality to adapt and remain meaningful over time. When ideas vibrate at this higher frequency, they inspire, motivate, and transform people and their perceptions. This notion is especially pertinent in fields where innovation and adaptability are paramount. A message that vibrates at a higher rate is one that stands out amid the noise, capturing attention and sparking engagement.

For those working in industries like management or entrepreneurship, recognizing the pivotal role of content can enhance strategic approaches to communication. By crafting messages that encapsulate enduring values and resonant themes, professionals ensure their ideas maintain relevance and effectiveness. Here, developing the narrative is key—it's about finding the essence that speaks universally while aligning with specific objectives. Crafting such content requires creativity and insight into both audience needs and the broader cultural context.

Moreover, creating value often involves giving more than receiving. Providing content that offers insights, solutions, and inspiration without immediate benefit furthers trust and connection. This approach is strategic, fostering relationships and encouraging reciprocation. By focusing on what the audience gains, communicators establish a reputation for reliability and respect, building a platform for sustained engagement. In competitive environments, being known for valuable contributions can distinguish individuals and organizations, enhancing overall effectiveness.

Choosing the right medium for your content is equally crucial. And emphasizing creativity and adaptability ensures content vibrates at a higher rate, elevating both personal and organizational communication efforts.

Access as a Gateway to Ideas

Navigating the dynamic landscape of communication in modern professional environments requires an understanding of how access influences the spread and impact of ideas. In a world where information flows freely and rapidly, recognizing the significance of access is crucial for ensuring that messages reach their intended audiences effectively. The extent to which ideas can move through networks is often dictated by accessibility, making it a fundamental pillar in successful communication strategies.

Access serves as the gateway through which ideas travel, determining both the scope and effectiveness of their journey to audiences. Imagine launching a new marketing campaign or rolling out an innovative product—without proper channels of access, even the most groundbreaking ideas may fall on deaf ears. Access ensures that ideas are not just spoken but heard, shared, and embraced. It allows professionals in fields such as sales, marketing, and media to connect with clients, consumers, and colleagues in meaningful ways.

As our universe continues to expand metaphorically, adding layers of connectivity and value, the distribution of ideas becomes even more intricate yet rewarding. Technological advancements and globalization have woven a fabric where borders blur, offering unprecedented opportunities for idea dissemination. A marketer in New York can now seamlessly collaborate with a team in Tokyo, sharing insights and strategies that resonate across cultural lines thanks to expanded access. This vast connectivity enhances the potential for innovation, fostering environments where diverse perspectives fuel growth.

However, success in leveraging access demands a paradigm shift—from a mindset centered on asking to one focused on offering. In professional settings, this translates to prioritizing value creation over mere transactions. By providing resources, knowledge, and support without immediate expectation of return, individuals and organizations build robust networks grounded in reciprocity and trust. These networks become fertile grounds where ideas can flourish, unimpeded by traditional barriers or gatekeepers. Offering opens doors and creates pathways for collaboration, enriching the exchange of ideas and enhancing overall outcomes.

Trust plays a pivotal role in facilitating access and reducing resistance. When trust is established, individuals are more willing to let down their guard, welcoming new concepts and innovations. This openness accelerates manifestation—the process by which ideas transition from thought to reality. Trust acts as a lubricant, smoothing interactions and encouraging a free flow of communication. In industries like advertising and entertainment, where creativity thrives on collaboration, trusting relationships enable teams to push boundaries and explore novel solutions without fear of friction or misunderstanding.

To nurture trust within your professional circles, consider several strategies. Active listening emerges as a powerful communication tool, fostering stronger connections and deeper understanding. Testing your listening skills regularly helps refine this ability, ensuring you genuinely comprehend the needs and aspirations of those around you. Additionally, practice listening while multitasking to maintain focus and engagement despite multiple demands.

By embedding these practices into your routine, trust naturally evolves, creating spaces where ideas can be shared with less resistance and more enthusiasm. People feel valued and respected when they sense genuine interest and attention, paving the way for open dialogues and fruitful exchanges. This kind of environment nurtures creativity, encouraging teams to move beyond conventional thinking and embrace innovative approaches to problem-solving.

Navigating Mediums for Effective Communication

In today's global landscape, communication is an intricate dance of words and mediums that transcends borders and cultures. As professionals, we often find ourselves navigating this complex web, particularly in fields like sales, marketing, and management. Effective communication isn't just about having a conversation; it's about transmitting messages clearly and convincingly across diverse platforms. The mediums we choose can significantly impact how our messages are understood, especially when cultural nuances come into play.

Cultural diversity introduces a myriad of challenges as it brings together various traditions, languages, and communication styles. A marketing campaign might resonate well in one region but fall flat in another due to cultural differences. Similarly, a message delivered through social media might be misinterpreted if cultural context is not considered. It's crucial for communicators to recognize these differences and adapt their strategies to ensure clarity and effectiveness. This means not only translating words but also understanding cultural symbols, humor, and etiquette to avoid miscommunication.

Moreover, age and technological disparities add another layer of complexity to efficient communication. In today's work environment, it's not uncommon to find a diverse workforce spanning multiple generations. Each generation has its preferred communication methods, ranging from the traditional face-to-face meetings favored by older generations to digital interactions via email or instant messaging preferred by younger ones. For instance, while a seasoned manager might value a detailed report handed out during an in-person meeting, a younger team member may prefer a concise update sent via a messaging app. Understanding these preferences is vital to bridge communication gaps and enhance productivity.

Furthermore, technology itself is continuously evolving, with new tools and platforms emerging frequently. Staying updated with these advancements is pivotal for maintaining effective communication. Professionals must be adept at selecting the right medium for the right message. Email might be suitable for formal updates, while videoconferencing could be more effective for brainstorming sessions. Adapting to these changes ensures that the intended message is not just heard, but understood.

Matching the efficiency of a medium with the vision you're trying to share is perhaps one of the most strategic aspects of successful communication. This involves not only choosing the tool or platform but also tailoring your message to suit that medium. For example, a visual platform like Instagram may require a different approach than a professional network like LinkedIn. The key is to ensure that the essence of the message remains intact and is aligned with the medium's characteristics. This alignment helps in making the message more relatable and easier to absorb, ultimately contributing to achieving organizational goals.

It's essential to remember, however, that despite the rise of digital communication, face-to-face interaction often holds unmatched value, especially in conveying emotions and intent. A handshake, a smile, or even the tone of voice can express sincerity and empathy, elements often lost in digital correspondence. In high-stakes negotiations or sensitive discussions, meeting in person can foster trust and understanding, leading to more meaningful outcomes.

Consider a sales pitch scenario: Presenting in person allows the salesperson to read body language and adjust their approach dynamically, creating a more engaging and personalized experience for the client. Such direct interactions can significantly influence decision-making processes and outcomes, highlighting the importance of human connection in an increasingly digital world.

Honing our ability to choose the right medium is imperative. It requires a balance of adapting to new technologies while appreciating the timeless value of personal interaction. Shifting from "No" to "How" in communication supports this transition by opening pathways for creative solutions and fostering a mindset of possibility. Instead of dismissing certain mediums outright, embracing their potential can lead to innovative ways of connecting and conveying messages.

Providing value first in our interactions is another crucial guideline. Whether it's a multimedia presentation designed to inform and educate or a simple email update, focusing on what the recipient gains from the interaction should be at the forefront. This approach not only enhances the quality of communication but also builds stronger relationships founded on mutual respect and collaboration.

The Power of Listening in Communication

It's funny how the people we love the most are often the ones we miscommunicate with the most. And it's not because we don't care—usually, it's the opposite. The closeness creates a deeper emotional investment, a stronger need to be understood. But that closeness can also make us more reactive, more defensive, and more likely to assume the worst. We want so badly to be seen and heard that sometimes we forget to really see or hear the other person.

I've seen it in my own family.

When my wife, Julie, lost her mother, the grief was sharp and raw. Her mom had been sick for a long time, and before she passed, she told Julie she wanted her to keep a particular keepsake. It wasn't anything flashy or valuable in a financial sense. But it meant something. It carried weight. It was a way for Julie to hold on to her mom—something tangible in the wake of such an enormous loss.

After the funeral, Julie's brother asked for that same keepsake. He wanted to give it to his fiancée as a tribute to their mother. From his point of view, it was an act of love. From Julie's point of view, it was a betrayal of their mother's final wishes. And just like that, what could have been a moment of shared mourning and unity became a wedge. Two people who loved the same woman, who were both hurting, suddenly found themselves at odds.

Here's the hard part: Neither of them was wrong. They were both grieving. They were both trying to honor their mother in the way they knew how. But they weren't really hearing each other. The pain they were carrying was speaking louder than their words.

That's the cost of poor communication—especially when emotions run high. It's not always about one person being right and the other being wrong. Sometimes it's about two truths crashing into each other. And when we don't listen with curiosity and compassion, those crashes cause fractures.

This happens in families. It happens in marriages. It happens at work. A comment gets misread. A gesture gets misunderstood. An expectation goes unspoken. And suddenly, the people we care about most feel distant, or worse—hurt.

Effective communication isn't just about what we say. It's about what we're willing to hear. It's about how we make the other person feel in the process of understanding them. Listening isn't passive— it's one of the most active things we can do. And it's one of the greatest acts of love.

In professional settings, we often prize the ability to speak clearly, pitch well, or persuade. But listening is just as—if not more—important. Active listening means being fully present. It means setting down distractions and focusing entirely on what the other person is trying to communicate. Not just their words, but their tone, their body language, the feeling behind their message.

Take a marketing team preparing for a big campaign. There are deadlines, pressure, egos, and opinions flying. In that environment, active listening is a superpower. The team member who pauses, who asks thoughtful questions, who reflects back what they heard to ensure clarity—they're the one who brings the temperature down and the quality of the conversation up.

On the flip side, distractions and multitasking undermine this skill constantly. Think of a sales executive who's glancing at emails while on a client call. That divided attention doesn't just lead to missed details. It communicates a lack of respect. And that can cost the relationship.

This is where mindfulness comes in. Choosing to be present is a habit—and it's a game changer. Whether in a boardroom, a kitchen, or on a Zoom call, carving out space to give someone your full attention transforms the dynamic. It allows trust to build. It allows truth to land.

And when in doubt, verify. Feedback isn't just for performance reviews—it's a real-time communication tool. Paraphrasing what someone said, asking clarifying questions, or simply saying "Let me make sure I heard you right . . ." can prevent costly misunderstandings and make people feel deeply seen.

But listening is also shaped by perception. What we hear is filtered through our own beliefs, experiences, and wounds. That's why empathy is so critical. In the story about Julie and her brother, the message wasn't just about the keepsake. It was about grief, legacy, memory. When we fail to account for someone else's emotional context, we can misread even the most well-intentioned words.

And that's true everywhere. A leader might give what they think is helpful feedback, but if their tone comes across as condescending, the message lands as criticism. A parent might offer advice to their child, but if the child hears judgment, the guidance is lost. Perception always shapes reception.

At the heart of all this is one truth: People don't just want to be heard—they want to feel understood. They want to know that what they say matters. And that only happens when we're willing to slow down and listen with our whole selves.

Whether in business, in families, or in partnerships, the ability to listen well is what turns communication into connection. It's what turns conflict into collaboration. And it's what turns misunderstanding into meaning.

Because, at the end of the day, communication isn't about winning or being right. It's about staying close, even when it's hard.

Adopting "How?" Over "No!" to Foster Connection

This subtle yet powerful switch opens up avenues for deeper connections and enhanced problem-solving opportunities. By exploring possibilities rather than closing doors, individuals foster an environment where collaboration thrives. For instance, when faced with a challenging proposal, a reflexive "no" might stifle potential innovation. However, asking "How can this work for us?" empowers team members to brainstorm and bring fresh ideas to the table, leading to solutions that might otherwise have been overlooked.

Embracing abundance isn't just about empowerment; it also encompasses accountability and empathy. In industries such as sports and entertainment or advertising, it's easy to get caught in the rush of individual achievement. Yet, true progress often stems from recognizing the shared journey of colleagues and partners. By embodying a mindset of abundance, professionals are challenged to look beyond their immediate benefits and consider how their actions resonate within the community. This approach nurtures accountability, where each person's success contributes to the whole. Moreover, fostering empathy allows teams to connect on a human level, understanding diverse perspectives and experiences, which is critical for creative fields like media and journalism.

The power of asking for help, as well as offering it, cannot be underestimated. This principle becomes increasingly relevant in competitive environments where the drive for self-sufficiency may overshadow collaborative efforts. When team members ask for assistance, it signifies trust and a willingness to learn, while offering help reflects a commitment to collective growth. Together, these actions maximize potential by pooling resources, expertise, and insights. It acknowledges the concept of oneness—that we're all part of a larger tapestry and our strength lies in unity. Imagine a marketing campaign where team members share their unique skills and viewpoints; the result is often a richer, more nuanced output than if tackled alone.

Value, connection, awareness, and recognition serve as motivational pillars in cultivating meaningful interactions. Professionals who prioritize these elements experience profound shifts in their work dynamics. Valuing others goes beyond mere appreciation; it involves actively seeking to understand and leverage individual strengths. Making authentic connections requires intentional engagement and openness to others' ideas, especially in an arena where different personalities converge. Awareness, in this context, means being attuned to the nuances of communication—recognizing nonverbal cues and subtleties that often speak louder than words. Lastly, recognition isn't merely about accolades but acknowledging effort, creativity, and growth, inspiring continued innovation and dedication.

When navigating conflicts or interacting with diverse personalities, guidelines become essential tools. Handling conflicts effectively involves active listening, empathetic responses, and finding common ground. Communicating with different personalities requires flexibility, patience, and the ability to articulate thoughts clearly while being receptive to feedback. These skills not only prevent misunderstandings but also build stronger, more respectful relationships across departments and organizations.

Final Insights

In this chapter, we explored the messiness and meaning of communication, the final and perhaps most challenging of our Four Great Truths to truly embody and live—especially when stakes are high and relationships are close. From professional dynamics to personal heartbreak, we saw how miscommunication doesn't always stem from malice. Sometimes, as with Julie and her brother, it comes from two people doing their best to honor the same truth in different ways.

When emotions run high, the instinct to be right or protect ourselves can override our desire to connect. But when we slow down and truly listen—with empathy, not ego—we create the space for understanding, healing, and deeper connection.

Guidelines

- Growth in communication happens in the learning zone—not the comfort zone, and not in anxiety.
- The people who feel heard are the people who stay connected.
- Your communication doesn't just land in words—it vibrates in how you show up.
- Great communication starts with generosity, not performance.
- The right message in the wrong medium gets lost. Match message to method with intention.

Key Takeaways

- Every conflict carries multiple truths. The goal of communication isn't to win—it's to understand.
- Difficult people are often our best teachers. They sharpen our awareness and stretch our skills.
- The most important words are often the ones we don't say—make space for what's unsaid by listening deeper.
- Communication is a daily calibration. Be mindful of which zone you're operating in: comfort, learning, or anxiety.
- Vulnerability, when paired with intentional communication, strengthens relationships and builds trust.

Ask Yourself

- When was the last time I really listened without trying to fix, defend, or respond?
- Which zone do I tend to default to: comfort, learning, or anxiety? Why?

- Who brings out the best version of me when I'm around them?
- When did I last show appreciation, not just say it, but feel it, for someone in my circle?
- What frequency am I broadcasting to the world? Is it one others are excited to tune in to?

No one gets communication right all the time. We miss cues. We make assumptions. We let ego slip in. But growth happens when we notice—and choose differently. When we stretch gently into the learning zone, when we check in with ourselves and others, when we lead with empathy and curiosity, we begin to communicate not just to be heard, but to connect. That's how we stay close—especially when it's hard. And that's what turns even the most difficult conversations into transformative moments of clarity, compassion, and alignment.

CONCLUSION

Building a Legacy of Integrity

Building a legacy of integrity involves navigating the complex world of professional relationships with a focus on core values. Recognizing that our social circles can have a profound impact on our personal and professional journeys is key. The influence of those around us often mirrors back our priorities and principles, shaping our actions and decisions in ways we might not immediately realize. As we immerse ourselves in environments filled with kindness, gratitude, accountability, and service, these values become foundational in guiding us toward success. This final section explores how selecting the right influences can be transformative, encouraging us to embed integrity deeply into our daily interactions.

In the upcoming discussion, we will delve into the dynamics of social influence and its role in shaping our ethical compass. By examining real-world examples and scenarios, this section illustrates how surrounding ourselves with individuals who embody positive values can significantly alter our paths. From the camaraderie that inspires ethical practices in sales to the diversity of thought that fuels creativity in marketing, the text highlights the integral connections between our social networks and our professional growth. Readers will discover strategies for cultivating a nurturing environment, fostering resilience through diverse perspectives, and building relationships that bolster both personal fulfillment and career advancement. With these insights, professionals from various fields will find the guidance needed to craft a meaningful legacy grounded in integrity.

The Influence of Your Circle

It's all too easy to succumb to ego and think of individual effort as the driving force behind success. However, often overlooked is the powerful impact our social environments have on shaping not only our careers but also our personal development. Understanding how these environments influence our journey can be a pivotal step toward building a legacy rooted in integrity. At the core of this understanding is recognizing that the people we surround ourselves with can significantly affect our values, attitudes, and overall growth.

Our social circles are like mirrors reflecting shared values and attitudes back to us. When we spend time with those who prioritize kindness, gratitude, and accountability, we're more likely to internalize these values. They become guiding principles that inform our decisions and interactions, both in personal and professional settings. For example, a professional working in sales might find themselves more inclined toward ethical practices if they are within a circle that holds honesty and transparency in high regard. This community influence fosters a culture of integrity that can be transformative. Aligning efforts with core values can alter the trajectory of a career. I know it has for me time and time again. And I bet it has, and will again, for you.

Choosing positive influences can be a game changer when it comes to motivation and achieving goals. Consider an entrepreneur launching a new venture. Surrounding themselves with peers who are ambitious, driven, and supportive creates a fertile ground for innovation and perseverance. These positive influences serve as a catalyst, offering encouragement during setbacks and celebrating victories along the way. The motivation drawn from such a network not only helps in navigating challenges but also fuels the passion required to sustain long-term projects. It becomes evident that the energy and attitudes of those around us seep into our psyche, impacting our determination and our ability to envision and achieve goals.

An important aspect of cultivating a beneficial social environment is embracing diversity in perspectives. In fields like marketing or advertising, where creativity is key, surrounding oneself with individuals from varied backgrounds can unlock new ways of thinking and problem-solving. Diverse perspectives challenge assumptions and introduce novel ideas that might otherwise remain undiscovered. Imagine a marketing team brainstorming a campaign: The blend of different cultural insights and experiences can lead to groundbreaking concepts that resonate with a wider audience. This kind of collaborative synergy is crucial for staying relevant and innovative in any industry.

Healthy relationships provide emotional support and resilience against life's inevitable challenges. In competitive fields such as sports or media, where the pressure to perform is immense, having a network that offers understanding and empathy is invaluable. These relationships act as a buffer, helping to manage stress and maintain mental well-being. For instance, an athlete dealing with intense competition may find solace and strength in friends or mentors who offer reassurance and perspective, reminding them of their capabilities and past achievements. This emotional backing is not just comforting; it emboldens individuals to withstand challenges and bounce back stronger after setbacks.

To navigate our social environments effectively, it's crucial to be intentional about who we allow into our inner circle. Surround yourself with people who inspire and uplift you. Seek out those whose values align with your own and who actively contribute to your growth and well-being. This doesn't mean avoiding constructive criticism or diverse viewpoints—in fact, welcoming constructive feedback is essential for personal development—but rather, emphasizing connections that reinforce and bolster your core principles.

Fostering Growth Environments

Creating spaces that promote personal and professional development is a foundational step in building a legacy of integrity. It's about fostering an environment where innovation thrives, and individuals are encouraged to take calculated risks. These are not just corporate buzzwords; they form the backbone of any successful organization. Spaces charged with optimism do more than lift spirits—they ignite creativity and fuel continuous improvement. When employees feel optimistic about their work environment, they are more likely to step outside of their comfort zones, explore new ideas, and drive innovation forward.

Consider a workplace where positivity permeates every corner. In such spaces, taking risks isn't seen as a gamble but as an opportunity for growth. This mindset can lead to breakthroughs that redefine industries. Think of tech companies where the culture hinges on "fail fast, fail often," allowing them to stride confidently into unknown territories because they know an innovative success could be just around the corner. The technology sector provides many examples of this approach, where optimism inspires teams to push boundaries and discover groundbreaking solutions, making once-improbable dreams a reality.

Beyond fostering innovation, creating supportive environments is crucial for skill development. Constructive feedback is a powerful tool when delivered in a nurturing setting. It transforms potential weaknesses into strengths and turns constructive criticism into learning opportunities. Imagine an employee working on a project who encounters challenges. If the environment is supportive, feedback will be targeted at enhancing skills rather than pointing out flaws, encouraging growth without fear of judgment.

Feedback loops in professional settings provide real-time insights, serving to guide employees toward better performance and more refined skills. When individuals receive actionable suggestions in a positive ambience, they become adept at addressing issues head-on. Moreover, they develop resilience, a key trait in adapting to the ever-evolving demands of the modern workplace. The right kind of feedback nurtures a cycle of improvement and empowerment.

Open communication is another cornerstone of environments that inspire trust and collaboration. A company culture that emphasizes transparency builds stronger interpersonal relationships. Employees who feel heard and valued are more likely to contribute their best efforts toward common goals. Open lines of dialogue encourage the sharing of diverse perspectives, sparking collaborative endeavors.

Within such organizations, trust acts as the glue binding teams together. When individuals can communicate openly, voicing concerns or ideas without fear of reprisal, mutual respect grows. Healthy communication channels break down silos, enabling cross-departmental teams to work seamlessly toward achieving their objectives. It's no surprise that businesses that thrive on open communication are often the ones leading industry changes and setting trends through collective intelligence and effort.

Intentionally designed physical spaces can also significantly impact productivity and morale. The layout of an office is more than just desks and chairs; it's a strategic element in workflow management and employee satisfaction. Consider how a thoughtfully arranged workspace can boost efficiency by facilitating better movement and reducing distractions. Collaborative spaces, quiet zones, and communal areas cater to different work styles, ensuring everyone can perform at their peak.

A well-designed environment goes beyond mere aesthetics. Ergonomic furniture, adequate lighting, and access to natural elements like plants or sunlight play a pivotal role in employee well-being. These factors decrease stress and fatigue, enhance focus, and increase overall job satisfaction. Companies investing in ergonomic solutions often report lower absenteeism rates and higher morale among staff, translating to improved business outcomes.

Moreover, these physical attributes of a workspace shouldn't overshadow the emotional and cultural aspects. A vibrant atmosphere that reflects a company's ethos and values resonates deeply with its workforce. Whether through artwork, inspirational quotes, or simply a relaxed setting, each element contributes to a sense of belonging and purpose, reinforcing the organization's commitment to personal and professional growth.

Providing guidelines for creating environments that foster growth and positivity can be instrumental. Leaders should prioritize crafting atmospheres that empower individuals and teams alike. Encouraging optimism, maintaining open communication, and designing conducive physical spaces are all tangible steps toward achieving this goal. By implementing these practices, businesses pave the way for enduring success, enabling their people to flourish, innovate, and contribute meaningfully.

Nurturing an Abundance Mindset

In a scarcity mindset our focus lands on what's lacking—be it time, resources, or opportunities. However, to build a legacy that truly lasts, one must shift from this limited view to an abundance mindset—a perspective that opens doors to greater potential and fulfillment. Embracing this mindset means training oneself to see possibilities where others see obstacles, which can transform both your professional and personal lives.

An abundance mindset isn't just a lofty ideal; it's a practical approach to navigating challenges. When you view the world through a lens of abundance, setbacks become setups for comebacks. Instead of seeing problems as insurmountable barriers, they are perceived as opportunities for growth and innovation. Consider a sales manager who, instead of lamenting a lost client, views the situation as an opportunity to refine strategies and improve services. This viewpoint allows for creative solutions and fosters resilience, key components in any successful career path.

Practicing gratitude is another powerful tool in nurturing an abundance mindset. By focusing on what we have rather than what we lack, our outlook shifts positively, enhancing overall well-being. A marketing executive might start each day by acknowledging achievements, both big and small, thereby setting a tone of appreciation that permeates the work environment. Such a practice not only boosts morale but also reinforces the belief that there is enough to go around. Studies have shown that gratitude increases optimism, and optimistic individuals are better equipped to handle stress and challenges effectively.

Intentionally feeding your mind with ideas that reinforce abundance, not fear, helps cultivate this mindset further. Surround yourself with positivity—books, podcasts, and mentors who embody abundance thinking. For instance, entrepreneurs who engage with networks that focus on success stories and innovation rather than failures create a mental framework conducive to spotting opportunities in adversity. It's about consciously choosing what occupies your mind. A guideline here would be: Actively seek content and connections that bolster an abundant outlook and shape your perception toward potential rather than limitations.

Moreover, embracing lifelong learning plays a critical role in maintaining an abundance mindset. In industries characterized by rapid change, like media and advertising, staying updated and adapting is crucial. Lifelong learners look at new information as an opportunity to grow rather than a threat to their current knowledge base. For instance, a journalist who continually hones research skills is more adaptable to shifts in digital media landscapes. This dynamic approach enables professionals to remain relevant and capitalize on emerging trends.

Resilience, too, is fortified when the focus is on growth rather than limitations. Understanding that failure is part of the journey to success empowers professionals to persevere. Take the example of an athlete who uses missed goals as motivation to train harder. By concentrating on development and improvements, rather than dwelling on shortcomings, resilience is nurtured. This growth-oriented mindset ensures that each setback is seen as a stepping stone to achieving excellence.

The notion of shifting focus from scarcity to abundance extends beyond individual benefits; it has profound implications for organizations as well. Companies embracing this philosophy foster environments that encourage creativity and collaboration. When team members believe there are enough resources and opportunities for everyone, competition gives way to cooperation. A management firm, for instance, that prioritizes shared success over individual winnings is more likely to cultivate loyalty and drive among employees, resulting in sustainable growth.

Building a legacy of integrity through an abundance mindset is a journey filled with continuous self-reflection and adaptation. It requires a commitment to see beyond immediate constraints and adopt a long-term vision where opportunities abound. By recognizing that the foundation of every endeavor lies in how we perceive the world, professionals are empowered to not only achieve personal success but also contribute positively to those around them.

Service as a Leadership Principle

In any competitive work environment, the essence of thriving as a leader lies in prioritizing the addition of value to others. This foundation creates a ripple effect that extends beyond business successes, paving the way for lasting relationships and profound impacts. Service-focused leadership, at its core, is about steering the ship with an unwavering commitment to put people first.

Firstly, let's delve into the idea that service-focused leadership inherently builds trust and loyalty among team members. By engaging in actions that genuinely consider the needs and growth of others, leaders set a precedent for how collaboration should function. Imagine a manager who consistently checks in with their team not only during crisis moments but also during times of calm. Their efforts in understanding team dynamics, personal challenges, and professional aspirations translate into a sense of belonging and security. When employees feel valued and heard, they are more willing to invest their energy and creativity back into the organization. Through consistent, deliberate actions, leaders can foster environments where trust isn't just earned, but naturally cultivated over time.

Extending this notion outward, value-driven interactions are key in establishing long-lasting connections with clients. Consider a salesperson who goes beyond simply pitching a product by listening actively to client needs and offering solutions tailored to meet those specifics. This approach not only enhances client satisfaction but also positions the salesperson as a reliable partner rather than just another vendor. Such meaningful engagements lay the groundwork for enduring partnerships, where clients see the relationship as an asset rather than a transaction. The focus on authentic communication and empathy ensures that interactions remain rooted in mutual respect and shared goals, further solidifying bonds without the need for constant renegotiation or reassurance.

Moreover, when leaders empower through service, they unlock pathways to sustainable success and influence. Empowerment doesn't mean relinquishing control; it means providing the tools and support necessary for others to thrive autonomously. For instance, a coach who provides athletes with individualized training plans while encouraging input from the athletes themselves fosters an environment of growth and self-improvement. As these athletes experience success based on shared effort and trust, the coach's influence expands, transcending the immediate goals to positively impact wider arenas. Leaders who embrace empowerment recognize that their legacy is built upon the collective achievements of those they uplift, driving forward momentum that sustains itself through inspired action.

Selflessness in leadership is a cornerstone that inspires followers to act with integrity. A leader's willingness to prioritize the needs of others above their own ambitions demonstrates a commitment to ethical conduct. Take, for example, an entrepreneur known for investing a significant portion of profits back into local communities through initiatives that promote education and sustainability. This act of selflessness not only enhances their reputation but encourages others within the organization to pursue similarly altruistic endeavors. Such examples create a culture where integrity is woven into the fabric of everyday operations, ensuring that decisions are aligned with core values and collectively beneficial outcomes.

Conducting Business with Integrity

Upholding ethics in business practices is essential for building a lasting legacy of integrity. At the heart of every successful organization lies the ability to make ethical decisions, as these choices shape both reputation and long-term success. When businesses prioritize ethical decision-making, they cultivate an environment of trust and respect, which ultimately benefits both the company and its stakeholders.

Consider a scenario where a business must decide whether to use sustainable materials instead of cheaper, environmentally harmful alternatives. By opting for the former, the company not only protects the environment but also establishes itself as a responsible entity. This commitment to doing what is right resonates with customers and can lead to a more loyal client base. Ethical decision-making like this forms the foundation upon which enduring reputations are built, encouraging others to follow suit.

Accountability in actions further underscores a business's dedication to integrity. When individuals within an organization take responsibility for their decisions and their outcomes—good or bad—they foster a culture of reliability and honesty. Personal accountability enhances credibility and sets a standard for professional conduct that others will be inclined to emulate. Owning up to mistakes and learning from them can transform potential setbacks into opportunities for growth and improvement.

For example, an advertising firm might face backlash over a campaign that inadvertently offended certain groups. By swiftly acknowledging the issue and taking corrective actions, the firm not only rectifies the mistake but demonstrates accountability. This openness can enhance the firm's credibility and reassure clients that the company values integrity over simply maintaining a polished image.

Transparent communication is another pillar that supports the structure of ethical business practices. Clear and open dialogue with stakeholders—be it employees, customers, or investors—reinforces trust and promotes engagement. In industries like media and journalism, transparency is especially crucial as it directly impacts public perception and trustworthiness. When businesses communicate honestly about challenges and successes, they humanize their brand and create stronger connections with their audience.

For instance, if a sports team encounters financial difficulties, transparent communication with fans and sponsors can rally support rather than erode confidence. Sharing plans for addressing the issues and inviting stakeholder feedback can turn a challenging situation into a collaborative effort toward recovery. Such transparency reflects a commitment to integrity and fortifies trust even in difficult times.

Aligning business goals with personal values is key to achieving holistic fulfillment, not just for the organization but also for the individuals who drive its mission. When there's harmony between what a company strives for and the values its leaders and employees hold dear, the work feels more meaningful and engaging. This alignment helps professionals in competitive fields like entrepreneurship or management to maintain clarity and motivation amid pressures.

Imagine an entrepreneur driven by a passion for innovation. If their business model prioritizes profit over ethical considerations or personal values, they may experience internal conflict that affects decision-making and satisfaction. However, when their business practices reflect their core beliefs—such as prioritizing customer well-being or environmental sustainability—they find greater purpose and fulfillment in their work. This alignment can inspire similar commitments from team members and partners, creating a cohesive and value-driven company culture.

In practice, this alignment may manifest as a media company choosing to invest in content that educates and empowers audiences rather than sensationalism for quick gains. The emphasis on generating positive impact aligns with the company's foundational values, ensuring that every business action contributes to its broader vision. This congruence not only leaves a lasting impact but also enriches the lives of those involved, reinforcing the company's integrity.

Ultimately, upholding ethics in business practices isn't just about doing what's right; it's about leaving a legacy that endures. Businesses that weave ethical decision-making, accountability, transparency, and value alignment into their fabric create a resilient and honorable identity. These principles guide interactions and operations, fostering environments where stakeholders feel valued and respected. Through steadfast commitment to these ideals, every challenge becomes an opportunity to reaffirm dedication to integrity.

Bringing It All Together

Reflecting on the elements of this book, it's evident that cultivating a fulfilling career and life rests upon values like kindness, gratitude, accountability, and service. These principles shape our interactions and guide us in our professional journeys. We've explored how the people we choose to surround ourselves with mirror these values back to us, influencing our decisions and actions both personally and professionally. Surrounding ourselves with positive influences can be transformative, acting as a catalyst for motivation while fostering innovation and resilience. This conscious effort in shaping our social circles underscores the importance of intentional relationships that align with our core values.

Embracing diversity and maintaining an environment open to varied perspectives enriches creativity and problem-solving abilities, especially in fields like marketing or entrepreneurship. Understanding that healthy relationships provide emotional resilience is crucial in navigating competitive arenas such as sports or media. They offer support amid challenges, creating a buffer that empowers growth and success. In essence, by intentionally crafting our social environments to reflect the values at the heart of successful businesses and lives, we not only propel ourselves toward our goals but also build a legacy founded on integrity and collaboration.

And if you need a reminder of just how powerful simple truths can be, go back to where this book began—with Leigh Steinberg, the Rams deal, and the words that changed everything: *Always be fair. Don't do business with dicks.* That wasn't just advice. It was a compass. It helped navigate a $900 million negotiation, but more importantly, it helped navigate life. Those principles are still my true north.

You don't need to be perfect to lead with integrity. You just need to keep showing up with kindness, gratitude, accountability, and the courage to surround yourself with people who bring out your best. Whether you're finalizing the biggest deal of your life or choosing who sits at your table, the real legacy you build isn't found in the numbers. It's found in the people, the energy, and the intention behind every decision. Choose wisely—and keep going.

It turns out, Leigh was right all along: The secret to success isn't being the smartest person in the room. It's being the kindest one with the clearest compass.

Acknowledgments

I would like to thank the following people for assisting me on my journey. First and foremost, my family. Especially my wife, Julie, Marissa, Mia, Marlena, Miles, and my mom, Karen—you are my number one nonnegotiables.

I also want to express my deepest gratitude to God, the ultimate source of light, love, and lessons in my life. Every part of who I am and what I do begins and ends with faith and gratitude for something far greater than myself.

To Albert Einstein, thank you for reminding us that imagination is more powerful than knowledge. You helped me see beyond what's in front of me and believe in what's possible. To Dr. Wayne Dyer, your wisdom still echoes in my life, especially in the moments when I'm tempted to judge or react instead of respond. And to Marshall Faulk, watching you lead on and off the field showed me what greatness really looks like. I've tried to carry that same standard into every room, every deal, and every decision.

To my team, past, present, and future, thank you. Whether you were with us for a day, a decade, or you're still on your way, you've shaped this mission. You've helped me build it, break it, rebuild it, and grow from it. I wouldn't be here without you.

To the mentors, friends, and teammates I didn't name, if you're reading this thinking, "Hey, what about me?" you're right. Thank you. I see you, and I appreciate you more than you know.

And finally, to the people who inspired the title of this book, you know who you are. Thank you for showing me exactly who I don't want to be. I mean that sincerely. Your example helped shape my values and, hopefully, this book helps someone else avoid the same mistakes.

About the Author

DAVID MELTZER is the Chairman of the Napoleon Hill Institute and formerly served as CEO of the renowned Leigh Steinberg Sports & Entertainment agency, which was the inspiration for the movie *Jerry Maguire*. He is a globally recognized entrepreneur, investor, and top business coach. *Variety* magazine has recognized him as their Sports Humanitarian of the Year, and he has been awarded the Ellis Island Medal of Honor.

David is the host of *The Playbook*, a top-ranked podcast featuring athletes, celebrities, and entrepreneurs sharing their playbook to success. He is also a featured Titan on *Go Fund Yourself*, the #1 show on Cheddar, where he helps everyday people fund their dreams. As Executive Producer of the Apple TV series *2 Minute Drill* and *Office Hours*, as well as Entrepreneur's #1 digital business show, *Elevator Pitch*, David brings unmatched insights to audiences worldwide.

He serves as Chief Chancellor of JA Worldwide, one of the world's largest and most impactful youth-serving NGOs, which has been nominated for the Nobel Peace Prize for its contributions to education and entrepreneurship.

David's journey has been featured in books, movies, and TV, including *World's Greatest Motivators*, *Think and Grow Rich*, and Netflix's *Beyond the Secret*. His life's mission is to empower OVER 1 BILLION people to be happy. This simple yet powerful mission has led him on an incredible journey to provide one thing...**VALUE**. In all his content and communication, that's exactly what you'll receive.